Oshkosh:
A South Sider
Remembers

D1453757

Ron La Point

First published by Dog Ear Publishing
4010 W. 86th Street, Ste H
Indianapolis, IN 46268
www.dogearpublishing.net

ISBN: 978-159858-511-7

This book is printed on acid-free paper.

Printed in the United States of America

Table of Contents

Acknowledgements

Without the gentle prodding of Ed Holladay and Dan Rylance this book would not have been published.

I chose Ed Holladay, a former teaching colleague and friend, as one of my first readers. I knew he would be methodical and fair in his evaluation. His kind assessment of the unfinished text provided me with the needed inspiration to continue.

Dan Rylance, a friend, a fellow golfer, a writer of books and a former newspaper editor, edited the final copy. His many annotations helped me overcome my fondness for wordiness and my attachment to semi-colons and long sentences.

To both Ed and Dan I owe a debt of gratitude.

Most of the pictures of Oshkosh were provided by Dan Radig, a south side resident, who has in his collection hundreds of photographs of 19th and 20th century Oshkosh. I am deeply grateful to Dan for allowing me to examine his collection and choose the ones I thought might enhance the composition of this book.

I also want to thank Joe Hemmer and Rick Karr, readers of an earlier manuscript, for their comments. And to my wife Carol: thanks for understanding.

Foreword

In this fast paced world of mind-boggling change and uncertainty, isn't it comforting to reminisce about a simpler time. For those of us in the fall of our lives memories of our youth recall a time more sanguine, a time when right and wrong had greater certainty and a time when our neighborhoods had a greater sense of community. Granted that sense of community sometimes stifled our adolescent adventures, but it always offered a safety net when life took a difficult turn.

Some would say we can't ever go back, but Ron La Point's <u>Oshkosh</u>: <u>A</u> <u>South</u> <u>Sider</u> <u>Remembers</u> refutes that notion. This literary effort is a treasure drove of memories and a marvelous gift to Ron's large, extended family. But it is also a significant gift to any of his contemporaries who were also children of the south side during the 1940s and 1950s. To the rest of us, who didn't share this experience, his odyssey of memories can be the catalyst to seek out our own origins and recapture some of the innocence and charm of a bygone era. Some would say it is latent to our nature to know who we are and from whence we came. If the notion has validity, Ron La Point has successfully scratched this itch.

As a former teaching colleague, I had the opportunity to share a profession with this man and he was known for his integrity, agile intellect, academic prowess and appreciation for the lessons of the past. His high regard for extended family and community that nurtured his youth was ever present. Ron brings all these attributes to this literary effort.

This book is a series of vignettes, the composite of which collectively tells the story of what many would call a childhood to envy. Neighbors, the schools, the intensity of adolescence games and the athletic prowess of his childhood friends are only part of Ron's memories. To read this book is to conjure memories of Hollywood's Bowery Boys. From marbles to baseball, the joy of friends and competition abound.

The secular world might have been full of fun and games, but Ron's introduction into the spiritual realm was a bit more stressful. The church of his youth, characterized by German ethnicity and the autocratic shepherding by an all too typical Herr Pastor, are experiences that escaped few of his contemporaries.

The mystery of parental politics, set in a post Great Depression, New Deal background, and the economic lessons learned picking cherries in Door County are only two segments of Ron's youth that are reflective of my own. An adult passion for a particular political persuasion and definitive lectures concerning economic strategies to survive in a time of scarcity, can be mystifying to a young boy whose interests do not transcend penny candy and sandlot baseball. These episodic reflections give this writer insight into the adult attitudes of a teaching colleague who shared my professional life.

Adulthood is often a time of traumatic discernment as we try to come to grips with an accurate portrait of our parents and their parenting adequacy. We live with a realization that our adolescent memories of parents were probably perverted by our struggle for autonomy and new experience. As adults we have a greater appreciation for the trials and tribulations of parenting. It is within this context that Ron shares moving portraits of his parents and captures the love, joys and pain of introspection.

There is hardly a single institution of that area and era that escapes his scrutiny. Oregon Street could satisfy almost all of anyone's economic needs. From grocery stores to taverns, meat markets to movie houses, Ron's memories breathe life into a commercial essence that predates the sterility of the contemporary strip malls.

For those of us who are immigrants to this city, <u>Oshkosh</u> : <u>A South Sider Remembers</u> can deepen our understanding and appreciation of Oshkosh. A strong work ethic, altruism born of a strong sense of community, love of family and an appreciation of the simples joys of life are legacies that add to the contemporary quality of life in this community.

Ed Holladay

Introduction

When asked how he came to write <u>The Land Remembered</u> in 1967, a book about his childhood and the land and the people he came to know, Ben Logan said: "It comes from a nagging sense of something unfinished, something inside me wanting to come out and play, some need to create a time I rushed through, too busy living to think about it, and a need now to look again, feel again, and try to understand the meanings of where and who I've been."

Logan's journey to his childhood home in the hill country of southeastern Wisconsin where he grew up in the 1920s and 1930s struck a nostalgic chord in his readers. Of the many letters he received, some wrote that his experience gave them courage to start a search to rediscover the qualities of those earlier days. Others told him of the special pilgrimages they made to the place of their birth, perhaps, as Logan points out, to find clues about the scattered pieces of their earlier lives. Most of the letters were filled with a yearning, a little-understood need to reach back, to complete some circle of life. So it is with so many of us; a need to understand the meanings of where and who we've been.

With a longing to return to my own past, I soon embarked on a journey of my own, a journey that took me to this place I once called home.

The place was Oshkosh, Wisconsin, located on the waterways of the Wolf and Fox Rivers and four adjoining lakes. It was at one time considered the wood capital of the world until the white pine in the northwoods gave out.

The pines of the vast Wolf River forests in northern Wisconsin were floated hundreds of miles downstream to the many saw mills hugging the Fox River dividing this city that drew its name from an Indian chief. The names of Paine, Sawyer, Radford, Morgan, Buckstaff and a host of other lumber barons still resonate in this place that was once known far and wide as "Sawdust City."

It was named after Chief Oshkosh, the leader of the Menominee Indians, a tribe, like so many others, forced to move west of the Mississippi River to make room for the surge of white migrants from the east. These early pioneers of the soil included my great-great grandparents William and Julissa Tritt who came from Ohio and settled a few miles west of Oshkosh 157 years ago in the woods of what is now the Town of Poygan. Four years following his arrival my great-great grandfather was elected Town Chairman later earning the title of Peacemaker by amicably helping to settle differences among the early settlers and the Menominee Indians who initially refused to leave their homeland.

With this ancestral stake in the area's history and my own abiding interest in the past, and a growing file of flashbacks as a beginning, I began this intensely personal journey that played out in the middle part of the last century.

I soon discovered there are few things more deceptive than childhood memories – the line between memory and invention is sometimes untidy – and in more than a few instances when my recollections needed a firmer hand I found a friend in the Oshkosh Public Library.

This collection of personal remembrances includes tales of my mother's conservative, hard-working, and church-going German background, and my father's musical roots, and his high-faluting, left-leaning French-Irish ancestry, and of their families who helped shape their lives. But most speak to the problems and struggles of childhood, adolescence, boyhood friendships, the road to maturity, and to this community of people and its institutions that were woven into the fabric of my youth.

Although there may be bits of local history in what you read, the reader would be best served to consider this simply as a story of a boyhood experienced and mostly remembered and the route this writer chose to go home again.

The Neighborhood

Top photo: Jefferson School is undergoing roof alterations. The year is 1948.
Juedes Grocery is across the street. Bottom photo: looking south on Ohio Street.
Sunlite Dairy, on the corner of Eighth Street, is on the immediate right.

Tenth Street

The south side of Oshkosh, south of the Fox River, where we lived, was primarily Germanic, inhabited by immigrants from Bohemia, Bavaria, Prussia, Slovakia and their descendents. Like most immigrant centers of the early twentieth century Oshkosh was a city of neighborhoods. Ethnicity and religion marked its boundaries, although during the early years of the 1940s those lines of demarcation had already lost their glow. The territorial battles that often erupted between the "fish-eaters" of the Bohemian, Catholic, Sacred Heart Hi-Holder district in the Knapp Street area and the dogmatic, righteous Lutherans to the east were now distant memories.

Tenth Street, five blocks south of the river, was one of many south side neighborhoods dotted with one and two-story clapboard, turn-of-the-century houses. Our family lived in the front apartment at 640 Tenth Street. It consisted of a kitchen, a small living room, two bedrooms, and a bathroom shared with the occupants of the back apartment. With no locks on either door leading to the bathroom it often was an embarrassing moment for the one caught sitting on the throne.

The neighborhood, like others close by, was within walking distance of jobs in the wood and lumber industry located along the Fox River which divided this city of 40,000. When I came on board in the midst of the Great Depression, the men, when they could find work in one of the local factories or in one of the new government programs, earned money stay-at-home wives were asked to stretch from one Friday to the next. Dad, in the mid-to-late-thirties, finally found full-time work with the WPA, a New Deal program, digging sewers for the city. The pay was low – at the start he was paid $12 a week – but it did pay the bills.

When the working men gathered in taverns throughout the city after a hard day's work, stories would inevitably be exchanged about low pay, long hours, and union "busting," evoking scenes from their father's and grandfather's time. The Woodworker's Strike of 1898 against the Paine Lumber Company was still not considered by many wearing a "blue collar" as "a time gone by."

When war came, with its attending jobs and overtime pay, Dad worked long hours as a machinist at the Bell Machine Company located across the bridge on Jackson Street. A feeling of prosperity soon filled the homes of those who now found themselves with full-time work, but disappointment came as well to those expecting change. Wartime rationing and scarcity saw to this.

Rationing and the conversion of automobile plants to military needs meant that walking or riding a bus downtown were the usual modes of transportation. Walking simply was the way of life for most, certainly for our family now numbering seven. A car was a luxury most families could not afford.

This was a time before shopping centers, super highways and parking lots. Within a two block radius of our house one could count one butcher shop, four grocery stores, two churches, one elementary school, and a commercial center where, when going from store to store, one actually walked on a sidewalk.

It was a different time, a less-hurried one, although the stay-at-home wives and mothers might object to such a notion. Still, as seen through the eyes of one not yet 10, it had its own pace, its own rhythm.

In most of the city neighborhoods trucks, large and small, could be seen on most days during the warm months shopping their goods or completing some municipal project. Farmers hawked their wares by hollering in a measured cadence, loud enough so their voices could be heard by women far up the street working inside their homes. Milkmen carried glass bottles of milk in wire baskets depositing those quart-size bottles of pasteurized milk and an assortment of diary products by the side door before the breakfast hour. The coal and wood deliveries made once or twice a year to those not yet able to afford central heating generated dust and debris as it made its way down the chute into the coal bin located in what was then called a cellar.

There were ice deliveries as well. When the ice man was spotted coming up the street on those hot summer afternoons delivering blocks of ice to houses without an electric refrigerator, he was greeted with an unbounded eagerness by the neighborhood kids. The ice chips and shavings made this a special time of our youth.

When city trucks carrying gravel and hot, sticky, liquid asphalt appeared on our street, my mother, knowing her children's curiosity and fully aware of her clothing budget, warned us not to get too close to their work. And on those hot summer nights when mosquitoes were thick and bothersome, the city sent out their DDT trucks to spray those noxious fumes not yet knowing the long-term effects it might have on the young.

I always looked forward to the Wonder and Omar bread men making their rounds introducing products to neighborhood housewives. With small loaves of bread to sample and the pitch that their product would stay fresh for days, the culture of bread-making in the home eventually lost out to boughten bread.

This was the age of the small grocery store and there were two within a block of our house. Juedes, on the corner of Tenth and Minnesota Streets won over Lorentzens on Ninth and Iowa for our limited purchases. Juedes was roomier, cleaner, and, more importantly for the 10 and under crowd, had a large glass encased candy counter filled with penny and two-for-a-penny candies. What a wonder it all was.

Living on our block were the Ratzburgs, Zilzes, Stephens, Ottos, Mauers, Weeds, Pankows, Raubes, Apels, and the Schmidts. Even Bill Goltz, the Chief of Police, lived up the street. But the favorite of the neighborhood kids still straddling the innocence of single digits was our across-the-street neighbor, Mr. Nimmar.

He was affectionately called Grandpa Nimmar by those of us who saw those kindly eyes wearing the same bib overalls and faded blue work shirt every day. When he invited us over to pick grapes or berries it was an adventure, almost jungle-like, to traipse through a backyard inundated with berry bushes and snarling grapevines that rapped around wooden poles lining the cement block walking path leading from his back door, and an overgrown garden that required more care than Mr. Nimmar was apparently willing to provide. One had to duck and dodge when you entered this oasis of unfettered greenery.

At those times Grandpa Nimmar sat on his front stoop or stood watching the neighborhood kids play, he would call us over and offer a pink or white candy lozenge recently purchased at Juedes. And just when we thought he was done handing out goodies, he would start digging in his many pockets, feel around, come up empty and frown, and then suddenly and with a twinkle in his eyes find an Indian head penny and say: "Who doesn't have one of these yet?"

This small neatly-packaged world of mine ended in the fall of 1944, shortly after my ninth birthday, when our family moved, four blocks away, to a house on Minnesota Street and to a neighborhood whose appearance and vitality was much like the one we had just left.

World War II

Together with the lingering effects of the Depression, World War II was the natural state of affairs during the early years of adolescence. Most every evening on our new Philco console, we would gather around and listen to Gabriel Heatter declare at the end of his broadcast: "And the sky over England is not yet in Hitler's hands."

In some ways these were happier times. Dad was working, money, if not plentiful, was not scarce, and we had beef roasts most Sundays, pork and beef when the butcher shop and the red tokens cooperated. My two older brothers no longer pulled their wagon to the corner of Seventh and South Main to pick up surplus foods, and Mother no longer feared the sound of the Relief Lady on our front porch.

Shortly into the war Mother received ration books and tokens. When she went to buy meat, butter, sugar, and shoes later on, she needed to hand over ration stamps or dime-like tokens along with money to buy the item.

Most everyone planted a vegetable garden. It provided fresh and inexpensive food and it was patriotic as it saved canned vegetables for our soldiers overseas. The bigger the garden, the greater the patriotism. In our neighborhood the Hielsbergs were the most patriotic.

They grew everything from sweet corn and potatoes to the usual assortment of lettuce, cabbage, peas, beans, tomatoes, onions, radishes, kohlrabies, and carrots. Melons were generally not planted because the adults knew the neighborhood kids would pilfer them before they got on the dinner table.

No one was immune from the war. It was in our comics, in our movies, in our songs. The radio was filled with it. Most evenings my parents listened to Edward R. Murrow from London and Gabriel Heatter in his New York studio updating their listeners on the progress of the war.

Wartime in the forties had a feeling of its own. Unlike wars since, World War II had a home front. Civilians felt the war and fought it too. They fought it by working long hours in war industries. They fought it at the dinner table, with the cars they no longer drove and in the things they did without. They fought it by buying war bonds, by growing Victory Gardens, by conserving and salvaging things previously thrown away. They fought it in their minds as patriots, and they fought it in the songs they sang. They deeply felt a sense of loyalty and responsibility to get the job done.

To help finance the war effort we bought war stamps that we pasted in a United States Savings Bond booklet. When the booklet was full – $18.75 worth – it could be exchanged for a $25 war bond. This piecemeal fashion of loaning money to the government allowed even poorer families like ours a feeling of helping save a soldier's life.

There were air raid warnings and blackouts during those early years of the war. The roof of the First National Bank on Main Street, the tallest building in the city, was used by civil defense workers as a lookout for spotting enemy aircraft. I'm not sure if any were spotted, but I do remember Mother turning off the lights and pulling down the shades in our living room during that first city-wide blackout. The sirens blared and the seriousness that filled the air made the moment feel eerie to a 7 year old.

Kids helped too, Honey Hielsberg and I, when we were trying to scrape up some spending money, went door-to-door asking for old newspapers, cardboard, rags, and metals and took them down to Block Iron and Salvage or to Pumps' on Tenth by the river. On a good day each of us would walk home with 80 or 90 cents in our pockets.

And then it all came to an end.

I was standing in the driveway of our Minnesota home on an August day in 1945 when the bells in the tower of St Vincent's rang nonstop and the city sirens blew and screamed with joy. I ran into the house to ask Mother what was going on. She told me the war was over.

The School Grounds

"Find something to do at the school grounds" was a common refrain in our house. It was a place Mother could shoo away her kids when they were bored, getting in the way or simply making pests of themselves, which in those long dog-days of summer happened more often than she cared to remember.

When we played touch football on the street with the occasional car or two honking or waiting impatiently to get through, Dad, home from work and attempting to get some rest after the supper hour, would open the front screen porch door and holler: "Take that damn football to the school grounds where it belongs."

That place was Jefferson School three long, softball throws away. It was called by different names by different people: the playgrounds, the school yard, the school grounds.

Most of the neighborhood kids simply called it Jeff.

When I arrived there, either because of my mother's prodding, my dad's bellowing, or on my own volition, I invariably had to wait for others to get up some kind of game. Since the playground directors frowned on kids tossing balls against the building, I often played a game of bean bag before my friends got there hoping to post the high score of the week.

Occasionally I challenged one of the directors, or they me, who themselves were looking for something to do, in a game of Battleship, or if it wasn't too hot, I might ask for a basketball and dribble it with the confidence I seldom displayed on Marty Anderson's South Park teams. I would practice my two-hand set shots and one-hand push shots at the far end of the school grounds that would, on rare occasions, pass through the small square openings in the monkey bars. This makeshift basketball court was located a few yards away and separated by a cyclone fence from the Dougherty residence.

Boots and Bill Dougherty, always on the lookout for a soft touch, someone to beat, would usually come out if they had nothing better to do and challenge me to a game of horse. Mary, the youngest of the brood, would tag along to offer sibling encouragement.

There were times when the monkey bars offered a poor substitute for the real thing, and when it did we walked across the street to the Garbe residence. Jim Lee, a persuader of notable skills, was our lead man in gaining access to one of the few houses in the neighborhood with a concrete driveway and a basketball hoop.

But the highlight of those summers was softball. The backstop, until it was moved due to neighborhood complaints, was on the corner of Tenth and Minnesota. The house on Tenth, with the bay window located directly behind the cyclone fence in left field, 200 and some feet from home plate, was the target for the long-ball hitters. When a pitch arrived on the thick part of the bat, triumph and hope were inescapable feelings as the 12 inch softball, still suspended in mid-air as you rounded first, cleared this once insurmountable barrier. Hearing the sound of the skinned-up, graveled-scarred piece of horsehide striking the side of the house and in some rare instances crashing through the bay window overlooking the graveled driveway caused everyone to run for cover.

Those games of rounders and choosing-up sides passed the time of day and helped prepare us for interschool play, the highlight of the summer softball program.

Roosevelt, Merrill, and Lincoln schools were the usual teams to beat. The westsiders, a team roughly comprised of the Friedrichs, Mohrs, Reques, Lufts, Peters, and Millers were simply too skilled to beat when they all decided to play. And when we faced Ronnie Peterman, a smooth throwing figure-eighter from Merrill, we knew we were in for a rough time.

But it was Lincoln beating Jefferson for the city championship that may have been the best of them all. Three of Lincoln's players" Dick Walgren, Jack Zellmer and Tom Boettcher would

Jefferson's entry in the city playground softball league play in 1952
and champion of the South
Side circuit, faltered in the grand play-off bowing to Lincoln,
North Side loop champions in two straight games.
The South Side players from left to right,
front row: Aaron Hardt, Robert Evert, DuWayne Bartel, and Roger Zander. Back
row, left to right: Don Evert, Ron La Point,
Bob Hielsberg, Jerry Stegemeier, Ron Zander, and Bob Werner

later play key roles for the State Fast-Pitch Champions, Wertsch Motors.

Those summers of youth ended when the three month summer vacations began fading into memory. Full-time employment and the 50 hour work week replaced sitting on those chain-linked swings across from the monkey bars sucking on a lime popsicle while trying to figure out the rest of the day.

Winters

During this time of earmuffs and frozen hair, golashes and wet mittens, and the constancy of a drippy nose, the warmth of our front room coal-burning stove took on extra meaning. Despite our occasional desire to stay in a warm house playing outside was encouraged. Six boys inside with nothing to do, clamoring for attention, was not considered the approach to a relaxed evening for our parents. So we found things to do outside. Snow ball fights, the never-ending battle to be crowned King of the Hill and ice skating were among those teenage staples we enjoyed.

The city began flooding ice rinks in December if the weather permitted, and it usually took four or five good waterings to make the rink at Jefferson School skateable. To hurry things along a few of us, eager to get the season started, helped the man in charge water on some of those cold evenings. When a storm rolled in we donned our skates, grabbed a shovel from home and helped remove the snow from the iced area.

A warming house was provided. It was located in a small basement room off the school's front entrance where wooden planks were laid down to protect the floor and provide a degree of safety for the skater. There were times, however, when we stumbled and fell in our attempt to avoid the space between the boards that seemed to grow larger as we hurried on into the night.

My first skates were the two-runner blades that strapped over my everyday shoes. Once I got over the initial skittishness and gained a sense of balance, I graduated to the real ones; hand-me-down hockey skates always a size or two too big.

One Christmas, to my delight, my parents surprised me with my very own steel-toed skates. Mother, always mindful of her limited budget and my ever-growing shoe size, announced, before I had a chance to take off my shoes and try them on, that they might be a little big. She suggested I wear a pair of heavy wool socks over two everyday ones to correct the problem. "This way they'll last a few years."

To avoid the embarrassment of changing in the warming room, I dressed at home and walked on low-lying snow banks. or if that wasn't possible, on frozen or ice-encrusted lawns hoping my wobbly ankles held up for the evening ahead.

After arriving on the grounds two short blocks away, I would skate around the rink once or twice looking to see who was there, and then send shaved ice in the air at anyone I wanted to impress skating that night.

Much of our skating, depending on the circumstance, was to get close to some good-looking girl. Some touching, brushing, a gentle push was, in our still young adolescent minds, making it with the other sex. Ending up in a snow bank with a girl by virtue of being at the tail end of a pump-pump pull-away game was something we all strived for.

But the most romantic and often unsettling activity was to hold hands with a girl you hoped was there that night, skate around the rink in full view of everyone and pray for bigger and better things to come.

The Hielsbergs

The Hielsbergs, who happened to be our backyard neighbors when we still resided on Tenth Street, was a family of highly competitive, athletic, adventuresome and, more often than not, hard-nose kids. There was always something going on over there, some kind of activity, something that usually drew my attention, our attention, for the Hielsbergs' had four boys who were close to the ages of my two older brothers and me.

Junie or Gents (his given name Elmer sounded too old to lay on this not-yet-teen), and Honey (he's grown up now and prefers the name Bob) were the two youngest Hielsbergs and playmates of mine.

Marbles was our game of choice. We placed our marbles in the large circle drawn in their grassless backyard and the three of us played until one was left with only his shooter. Despite my reputation as a good player or maybe because of it, Junie and Honey, ganging-up in tandem, smirking and laughing as they set each other up, beat me more times then I care to remember. Eventually marbles gave way to games of stickball, softball, card playing and rubber gun fights.

It was those rubber gun fights that proved to be a turning point in our relationship. Automobile and bicycle inner tubes after the war were again made from real rubber, a substance that was durable and stretchable. We soon found use for the discarded ones.

We fashioned guns from blocks of wood purchased each year by their aunts' Elsie and Emma Hielsberg who lived next door. The cut notches in the soft wood were made at various lengths depending on the patience and one-up-manship of the designer. Junie and

Honey, and their cousins Marv and Kenny Hielsberg from Nebraska Street, were the best at this.

Junie and Marv seemed to glory in making the most sophisticated ones. The machine-like guns they turned out would soon be turned on the three of us. When they stretched the cut rubber onto the last notch of their weapons, the glee of satisfaction could clearly be seen on their faces. We knew then that they were ready for war. And those two were mean! They took extra pleasure in inflicting pain. When the battles were over the losers were taken prisoners, and losers were tortured on Ninth Street.

They usually began by tying us up with clothesline rope, draping the three of us over wooden horses, telling us what they had in mind, and getting immense satisfaction from our grimacing and yelping with pain. They played for keeps while Kenny, Honey and I were always thinking it was just a game.

One afternoon the three of us, finding ourselves alone, climbed their aunt's apple tree to have an apple eating contest. Everything was a contest with the Hielsbergs. No matter what we were playing or doing there always had to be winners and losers. I ate 33 of these small green apples that day using plenty of salt in my shaker while coming in last. Honey ate 37, and Kenny, showing his winner's smile as we climbed down, polished-off 39.

At the age of 9 or 10 Honey and I decided to take up smoking. Corn silk was the "tobacco" of choice. We went to his garden – the only one in the neighborhood that grew corn – and searched for the darkest and driest corn silk. We learned this from our older brothers who had done this before.

Finding what we were looking for we went directly to Elsie and Emma's outhouse. As we puffed away we noticed, through the crack in this small, airy building, that Junie and Marv, with conspiratorial smiles on their faces, were sneaking up on us. They must have seen the smoke curling out of the small openings in the wall. We knew they would take great satisfaction in turning us in so we made a run for it.

We raced through our backyard onto Tenth, Honey running one way, I another. The two soon grabbed us by the collars and marched us home.

Our parents dismissed it as part of growing-up.

Later on Honey and I decided to comb the streets for cigarette butts. We found the most success later on by the Cellar Tavern two doors down from our house on Minnesota Street. Stuffing the longer ones without lipstick stains in our pockets we began the walk back to Honeys'. Although the Hielsbergs had previously demonstrated the art of the deep inhale, the cigarette butt I lit and began smoking, as we trekked back to Ninth Street, made me dizzy.

As fate would have it we didn't make it to the outhouse that day. A friend of Mrs. Hielsberg spotted us puffing away while on our way to his house.

This time our parents decided enough was enough.

Nicknames

Nicknames were as common as green apples and a salt shaker on a summer day. Names like Wiener, Honey, Teamer, and Honky rolled off our tongues with a regularity that speaks to youth. I was tagged by some with an epithet appropriate to my sense of, let us say, correctness: Lip or Lippy. Others were tagged with Gents, Latchit, Donky, Smiley, Legs. My brother Ralph was Curly, his best friend Joints.

There was a feeling of intimacy, of being closer to the person who had a substituted name. Epithets were often used, but any moniker was accepted as a badge of admission as long as there was a sense of fair play.

For reasons now obscure we attached baby at the end of everyone's name, as in Bobby-baby or Honky-baby. If, for example, we were just sitting around Ole Menzels drinking Pepsi with our Planter's peanuts, I might say, just to break the ice, "hey, Donkey-baby." Donkey, with a smile, would replay in kind. That was it. But it was always good for a few laughs.

There were few people in our crowd called by their baptismal names. Their first name was either shortened or an ie or y added on. My brother Richard was called Rich or Richie, seldom Richard or Dick. His brothers preferred Rich. Brother Bob had more options. Abbreviated or extended versions of his name were Rob, Robbie, Bob and Bobby. He was called Bob by his friends, while the girls, who thought he was cute, called him Bobby.

If the baptismal name could not be shortened or extended with an ie or y, we usually used the last name in similar fashion.

Wayne Tauschmann became Tausch, Gerry Steinhilber, Steinie, Darrel Schmidt, Schmitty, and so it went. Wayne Reese was an exception. One could not do much with either of his names.

Oregon Street

It was the second largest commercial center in town and, if you were to count, nearly one hundred businesses lined this bustling corridor. It may not have been Main Street with its fine hotels, tall bank buildings and large department stores, but it was familiar and it was close by.

Like other commercial centers, it soon lost out to the dynamic engines of progress. The interstate system of highways that helped accelerate the country's economic growth also had the unintended consequence of slowly strangling the Oregon Streets to death. The changes came in increments but they came. By the 1980s this commercial corridor was teetering on the brink of collapse.

It was sad to watch

It was in this house on Minnesota Street, one block west of Oregon, where I awoke each morning to the sound of the clock tower bell of the neighboring church. It tolled every 15 minutes and could be heard by all good Catholics of St. Vincent's parish, even by some nearby Lutherans. The bell served as a wakeup call on school days and a reminder when playing at the school grounds, two blocks away, that we no longer had a good excuse for being late for the evening meal.

St. Vincent's was the focal point, the tallest building on this street that trumped in retail trade. When I was on an errand or just roaming the neighborhood, I often saw these strangely garbed women in black and white smiling and chattering before entering the side entrance of their church. When I did, I thought about venial and mortal sins, rosary beads and confessional booths, and most everything else that seemed strange and exotic about the Catholic Church to this boy about to be confirmed in the Missouri Synod of the Lutheran faith. I wondered then whether everything I heard about the Catholic Church was true.

St. Vincent's Church

As I past the church and continued on my way, I kept seeing what was no longer there. The buildings– most of them – remained but with new signs, new owners, new purposes. I saw what stood there now and I saw what went before.

Across the street from St. Vincent's I spotted the buildings that once housed Schuster's Shoe Repair and the Wigwam. Shoes were usually soled and heeled once, sometimes twice before our mother would march us down to Rothenbachs on Ninth for a new pair. The smell of leather and shoe polish, and Mr. Schuster speaking above the hum of the machine saying: "That'll come to two dollars and twenty-five cents please," brings back a sense of proportion.

The Wigwam, formerly Beernstsen Candies, now Oaks Candy, was an ice cream, soda, candy, sandwich kind of place. It was also a teenage hangout with booths, tables, and a nickel pin ball machine that tilted easily. Together with the Sugar Bowl, formerly a tavern owned and operated by Leroy "Lefty" Edwards of Oshkosh All Star fame, they were perfect places to squirm in our seats as we tried to get acquainted with some of the new girls from South Park Junior High.

Oregon Street 1944. Krogers on the corner of Ninth would soon move to a larger facility on Eighth.

The grocery stores on Oregon, with the exception of Krogers on Eighth were small usually family owned which was the case with most every business located here in the '50s. They existed and often prospered by offering a service not offered by the larger stores or they specialized in things like meats and fresh produce, fine cheeses, distilled beverages, and friendly service. Those that survived found their place, their special niche in a market that would soon be dominated by the larger chains

Meyer and Sons, an incredibly small store with its produce displayed out front, had its own loyal following, as did most of the other small grocers up and down the street. But only Friedrichs, Wickerts, Otto's Food Shop, and Biebels survived the '60s.

Wickerts on 17th, Friedrichs on 15th, and Ottos on 16th were specialty shops. Wickerts with its large potato bin outside and free delivery service; Friedrichs with its freshly cut meats, cut while you wait, and; Ottos with its ample supplies of alcoholic beverages sold at cut-rate prices attracted the faithful. Ottos was a good place to get cold meats and cheeses, a case of Peoples, and sample the wit of Don Wegener who was the main reason many shopped at the store owned by Kelly Otto.

Jimmy Pollnow (even us kids called him Jimmy), the owner of the Acee Deuce Bar and Bowling Lanes on Fourteenth, allowed us, who were not yet of legal age, to play cards, drink a pop, sometimes even tip a beer on those long-ago Saturday afternoons. It was not uncommon for the beat cop to walk in, chat with Jimmy, look around the premises, and not seeing anything untoward, give a tip of the hat and walk out the door leaving our hearts fluttering.

Haberkorn's Bar, formerly Norkofsky's Tavern, between Ninth and Tenth, was a regular stop for many of us after a ballgame. Ben, the owner, was cordial and didn't mind us coming in under the legal age. He also had one of the best shuffleboards in town with a surface so finely honed that it took little effort to guide the puck to the proper place.

There were other taverns with names like Carol and Dick's, Mary's, Witzke's, Muza's, the Polish Corner, and the Elbow Room that catered to most anyone who behaved and could put the proper change on the bar.

I often found myself sitting on the concrete steps of Siewert's Grocery eating a popsicle after playing basketball at Jefferson School; looking and sometimes buying an Ink Spot record at Ludewig's Record Shop; watching the up-and-coming Floyd Patterson scoring a quick KO on the Friday night Gillette fights at Harold's Bar after a night of bowling at the T&O, and; entering Meyer Brother's Jewelers to see what Doug and Rock were up to, and wondering whether they could fit a ring in my tight budget.

Oregon Street looking north in the 1920s. South side branch of
the public library is on the left

Time and again I was forced to listen to the owner of Jensen's
Barber Shop and his son belittle Charlie, an older man, with his
bulbous nose and his mental shortcomings while I sat in one of
their four barber chairs for my monthly 50 cent haircut. Charlie
lived on the site in exchange for performing a few menial tasks in
the shop and being the unwilling target for the biting remarks that
too often came his way.

Occasionally I would go with a friend to George Koch's Shoe
Repair so he could check if his daughter Barbara was there. Later
on, when I too became enamored with the other sex, I would
saunter into Mike's Grill, find out if she was working, and if she
was, play "Sleepy Time Girl' on the juke box.

Oregon Clothing, the premier clothier on the south side, was where my first suit, my confirmation suit was bought, although I don't hold that against them. Mother, frugal because she had to be, must have decided that the suit, even if it was a size too big, would last through some of my growing years.

Rothenbach Shoes, next to the south side branch of the public library, had an untarnished reputation for standing behind what they sold. It was a family operation, a friendly place to be, and a place our mother trusted to outfit all of her boys.

There were other businesses on Oregon. Places like the Banner Store, Hirschberg's, Menzel's, Havemann's, Gudden's, Rohner's, Jug Murphy's Mobil, Rudy Meyer Shell, and Mueller Potters, names that would stir the memory pot for many, but to me they were mere acquaintances, once-in-awhile neighbors, not the close friends I learned to cherish.

Oregon Street looking north in the 1960s

These places are mostly gone now. Less than 20 remain, most with different owners, some with different names. Oregon Street is no longer the center of commerce I once knew. The center, long ago, was rerouted to the west.

Schools and Such

Top photo: Jefferson School in the early 1900s.
Bottom: Jefferson School in the 1940s

Jefferson School

It was built in the late nineteenth century and named after Thomas Jefferson, the author of the Declaration of Independence, who later became our nation's third president. The building was an imposing structure, and, with the exception of the nearby Catholic church of St. Vincent's, three blocks removed, the tallest building as far as the eye could see.

My introduction to Jefferson School came September of 1939 when my mother walked me that one short block to introduce me to the Kindergarten teacher, Miss Miller, a neighbor lady who lived down the street. I was told, as we waited patiently in line, that she would be my teacher for the next two years.

On one of those first mornings of class she asked: "Is there anyone who can count to 100?" I raced up to her desk and waved my hand, over the many that rushed up with me, and amid the din, told her that I could count to 1,000. Like so many others in this classroom of four year olds I was eager to please.

That incident and others are recalled and teachers remembered during those eight years that started with finger painting and coloring between the lines, and ended with our sixth grade teacher's admonishment that we not disappoint her in the fall when studies began at South Park Junior High.

There was, for example, Miss Fleming's warnings, threats actually, to her first graders that promotion to second grade would not happen unless we could recite the alphabet from memory and read our first grade primer without stumbling over the words.

During milk break on Fridays in Miss McCullough's second grade classroom, we lined up to take our goiter pills from the large glass bowl she kept on her desk. We were told to chew the tablet while drinking our milk. The pills were taken to help control the size of one's thyroid glands that had troubled the previous generations.

Miss Weismueller, the fourth grade teacher, was everyone's favorite. She loved kids and treated them as if they were her own. She always wore a smile and nice words rolled off her lips as easily as softballs came off the bat of the best hitter in sixth grade, Sheeny Meyer. She even gave hugs if she thought you needed one. Unsettling as it was to us advancing third graders, Miss Weismueller became the third grade teacher when our class moved on to fourth.

Miss Cowan, a spinster (they were all unattached in a married sense as I think back), was our fifth grade teacher. She had the reputation of hitting the knuckles of your hand with a 12 inch wooden ruler when you were caught not paying attention, which, if memory serves, happened often during the afternoon hour she spent on fractions and decimal points.

One of the big disappointments in my yet young life occurred in Miss Randall's sixth grade class.

The selection of the sidewalk crossing guard was the crowning achievement of a sixth grader, even headier than a row monitor or being asked to fill the inkwells or distribute the mid-morning half-pints of milk. Strapping on that white belt with the patrol badge as a permanent patrol boy was an honor handed out to just a handful of students.

On the day selections were announced in front of the entire class the disappointment of not hearing my name called was only made worse when two girls were among those given this highly cherished badge of honor.

And all the while I thought it was just for boys!

Our school principal was Miss Nolte, an imposing woman with white hair and a manly haircut. She took a no-nonsense approach with kids who misbehaved, and when she entered a room or patrolled the hall during break time we minded our manners.

There was in addition to grades Kindergarten through sixth grade, a classroom set aside for those less-able to negotiate the traditional class offerings. It was called the Opportunity Room, one of many past and current euphemisms used to describe those challenged in the classroom.

Occasionally one of our teachers would take us on a field trip to this room on the second floor. I'm not sure if this was meant to be a warning to the loafers and mischief-makers among us or simply meant to round-off our education, but I was ill at ease when we did this. Awkward and self-conscious, I came away from these sessions not always knowing what to think or how to feel.

The students in this equal opportunity class were taught the skills to operate and maintain the weaving mechanism of this wooden frame of moving parts to be used, I assumed, to find work, to qualify for jobs in the community. To me this seemed, even at a tender age, so incongruous, so out of date, suitable more to the nineteenth century of our working grandparents.

The Jefferson School I once knew is gone now. It was leveled nearly a decade ago and replaced with a building both elegant and functional. It's a celebrated structure, one the community is proud of.

But I noticed things missing the day I drove by. The small asphalt diamond home to our sixth grade softball team was no longer there. Nor were the monkey bars and the chain-link swings we played on as we whiled away lazy summer days. They disappeared as well. Nowhere in sight was the stone pedestal we climbed that mounted the discolored and weathered face of the school's namesake. That was gone too.

Later that afternoon when I parked my car nearby to take a closer look, I wondered about time and place, and about things seen and unseen. I thought of this school that was no longer there, of my childhood friends, of kickball during recess, of the ice rink we helped flood, and all those summer days waiting for things to happen. I thought of all this as I lost myself in a quiet reverie.

And then, as if from the echo chambers of the past, my reverie was interrupted by the sight and sounds of seven strangely dressed women walking down the steps of the side entrance of this old stone edifice of my childhood chatting, smiling and waving as they began their daily trek home.

South Park Junior High

I got up early that morning, too excited to stay in bed, and dressed in newly purchased clothes I laid out the night before. It was the standard issue of the times: a pair of jeans (we called them overalls), a white tee shirt, white sweat socks, and newly acquired tennis shoes.

Bouncing excitedly down the steps from my upstairs bedroom, I quickly grabbed something to eat and walked those five blocks not wanting to be late.

When I arrived at school I saw a group of students buzzing with excitement as they milled around the side entrance. I casually walked over and noticed official-like papers posted on the outside of this double glass door. After easing myself to the front, close enough to see what the hubbub was about, I noticed an alphabetical listing of students matched with their homeroom teachers. I didn't yet know what a homeroom teacher was but discovered I was assigned to a Mr. Krahn.

Mr. Herbert Krahn did not smile much that first day. He was older and appeared as if he had gone through this first-day routine many times before. He showed little patience with our questions and general uneasiness and a 12 year olds' penchant for not listening.

The homeroom orientation didn't last long and when Mr. Krahn instructed us to follow our classroom schedule for the remainder of the day we were dismissed to attend our first hour class.

It was shortly into the term, more than likely the first week, when an episode brought me in direct contact with the principal, Mr. Reimer.

During one of those first homeroom periods Mr. Krahn instructed me to take the daily attendance slip to the office. As I entered and approached the counter to hand the secretary the slip, Mr. Herbert Reimer, for no apparent reason – not apparent to me anyway – stormed out of his inner office, and in a voice I thought everyone in the school heard, asked me, demanded to know, what I was doing there. I froze in place, too frightened even to answer. He said if he ever saw me in this office again he would put me on a week of detentions.

Speechless, never once uttering a word in my defense, I quickly walked back to the to homeroom and Mr. Krahn. Welcome to seventh grade and South Park School I thought. I made sure I stayed out of his way and out of the office for the duration of my stay.

I recall most of my teachers: Eddie Wichman, Robbie Robertson, Minnie Wegner, Lorraine Oaks, Marcille Simms, Seraph Kaprellian, Merrill Lewis, Frieda Klouda, Herbert Krahn, Dorothy Unger, and, most everyone's favorite, Marty "Andy" Anderson.

Class of 1950

Andy taught phy ed – we called it gym – and he coached most boy's sports. He was from the old school. We did it his way. Misbehavior was not tolerated. Whenever he needed to correct us, he did without hesitation or reluctance. A few others in the profession were from the same school of thought, but, unlike most others, Andy cared. He was the good father dozens of young boys never had at home.

Andy coached basketball and usually conducted himself with a deportment to be envied, even though, like most every coach, he wanted his team to win. His even demeanor, however, was always tested at semester time.

Up until 1953, there were mid-year graduation classes. The last of those January graduates, all members of a highly successful starting lineup, moved on to the next grade at semester break. This left Andy with a sizeable drop-off in talent for the last half of each season.

The system paid dividends for a few of us, but it was not part of the season the coach looked forward to. I often saw him shaking his head at our play, and once I overheard Mr. Seraph Kaprellian, an eighth grade science teacher, asking who he was going to start at guard in ninth grade: "I suppose La Point and Laatsch again, I don't have anybody else."

Our team play was spotty. Teamer Hansen was often a bright spot, sometimes the only one on those mid-year teams. Steve Youngson was a good player in ninth grade and his play gave Andy some satisfaction. Honky Demler made a hook shot now and then, and Donnie Laatsch, firing shot after shot, occasionally banked one in. Gary Parsons traveled too much bringing up the ball to be effective, and I remember scoring seven points against St. Marys in their gym as the highlight of my junior high career. And that pretty-much sums it up.

There seemed to be a love affair between Miss Simms and Mr. Wichman during our stay at Park. I don't know how serious it got, or if it even got off the ground, but they were good sports about the teasing they received.

There were others on the faculty that left lasting impressions. Robbie Robertson, an eighth grade social studies teacher, ran his class like basic training. Unlike Marty Anderson, he didn't appear to like kids. "Sit up straight pleeeeeeeeese, or else I'll have to come over there and sit you up myself."

His classroom was on the third floor and he patrolled the stairway on the north side of the building like a drill sergeant. If he caught you running up the steps or taking more than one step at a time he would holler: "You, you with the curly hair. I want you to walk down to the first floor slowly and then take the steps in a mannerly fashion." And after you did this he would give you that open smile that showed his separated teeth: "Now that wasn't so bad, now was it."

Later on, after he retired, I got to know Mr. Robertson and his deportment was much different. Of course, he was no longer dealing with a bunch of pubescent kids on a daily basis.

I enjoyed Merrill Lewis and the Boy's Chorus. The chorus was a four-part all-male group unique to Oshkosh and much of the state. There were tryouts and new uniforms, and there was pride in being a member, a pride instilled by the director whose dedication to music education in Oshkosh is widely known.

There was always a rush between classes to claim part of the bathroom mirror. Many of us, feeling the beginnings of manhood, wanted our hair to look just right for the girls in the next class.

Donnie Laatsch, Gary Parsons and I took it a step farther than most.

We had the highest and most overworked pompadours this side of Eugene Kempinger. We ran water through our combs to freshen up our waves in front that we thought all the girls admired. The reflections of the three of us looking in the mirror, making sure we looked exactly right, then wiping away the excess water dripping down the side of our faces before rushing to our next class is still one of the clearest memories of those days and one I no longer fawn over when viewing long-ago class pictures.

Those years at Park were my favorite years in school despite the run-in with the principal, and the time Marty Anderson accused me of smoking the night before I struggled in my attempt to pass the swimming pool's deep end test.

I'm still wondering who told him.

Oshkosh High School

It was in Room 410 of the old Red Brick building that we met those first 15 minutes of each day. Mr. Steffenson, our homeroom teacher and a student-kind-of-a-nice-guy, let us visit as long as the neighboring classrooms of Miss Kratsch and Miss Ledwell did not complain. He did not even seem to mind if we caught a few winks interrupted by a late night out.

The high school facility in the early 1950s was located in the heart of town on Algoma Boulevard and consisted of five interconnected buildings. The Main and Red Brick – where most of the academics were held – were connected to the other three by a tramway that allowed an unfettered flow of traffic during times of inclement weather. It was in this tramway where I first began noticing those fully developed high school girls promenading their wares.

High school for many of my friends and me was more of a passing phase, an ordeal to be borne, than a stepping-stone to an academic world waiting to be explored. So we fumbled our way through.

There were a few classes along the way that stood out among the many that did not. A Cappella Choir was one. Under the direction of Fred Leist it was considered one of the finest choral groups in the state. The annual operettas and community programs and the fact that I met a few cute girls from the east side made this one of the most pleasant and ennobling experiences of my high school days.

Oshkosh High School

During one of our rehearsals, in the fall of my sophomore year, a middle-age woman, a visitor I assumed, appeared in the choir room. After talking briefly to Mr. Leist, she turned and faced the class. Slowly looking around, checking faces, her gaze finally stopped at the far end of the fourth row.

I was soon asked to step out in the hall and it was there where I first met Olive Davenport, the high school drama coach.

She asked if I would like to be in a school play being cast. She was searching, she said, for students to play the younger children in the year's high school performance of "Cheaper by the Dozen." It turned out that Wayne Rosier and I, two faces not yet mature beyond junior high and untested in thespian waters, got two of the parts.

But highlights were few in this school too large and unwieldy for the average and not-so-average student. Being without well-defined goals school often got in the way of other, more important pursuits. But unlike my friends, I joined up with some of these same teachers as a colleague some 15 years later, I would think, to their consternation and bewilderment.

There were, among those on the staff, a few unforgettables: Rex Hess, the spinner of tall tales, delighted in his hunting and fishing stories and of his cottage in the northwoods. His reliance on the <u>Weekly</u> <u>Reader</u> each of those Fridays worked to perfection as it deflected the notoriously boring reading assignments in our U.S. History textbook. On the third floor of the Old Red Brick building was the animated and likeable Annabel Wood who, when pitching the annual oratory contest with her usual flair and unchecked enthusiasm, often forgot on those days to check homework assignments. And who could forget the jovial and light-hearted business teacher, Howard Pennewell, whose unwavering love of life gave us a sense that goodness often came in small packages.

There were others on this staff that left lasting impressions. Dick Maleszewski who carried the brunt of the teaching load in printing class worked harder than his contract may have called for while his associate, the indefatigable E.J. Bauer, never seem to tire of telling stories to anyone willing to listen.

But it was the perpetually non-smiling Ruth Ledwell for whom I often felt sorry. She couldn't understand why every student in this class of daily underachievers and mischiefmakers was not interested in dissecting a frog drenched in formaldehyde.

I skipped school once if I were not to count the times I told my mother I was not feeling well enough to attend classes.

It was in my senior year when I decided it was time. This was not something one did casually. A written excuse had to be hand-delivered to Hugo Radtke, Dean of Boys, the morning of your return. And Hugo had the reputation of disarming even those experienced in these ways.

It was a matinee running at the Time Theater, a movie about Abe Saperstein and the Harlem Globetrotters that I chose for my unveiling. As I sat in back checking everyone who entered the theater that day, my thoughts were not on the film but on Mr. Radtke or one of his associates who might walk in and put me on a week's worth of detentions.

The following morning as I nervously handed the Dean of Boys my excuse, forged in my mother's name, he looked at it, then at me with those penetrating eyes, giving me that knowing look of his, and then, much to my surprise, wrote out an admittance slip for the day's classes.

Admittedly, I had little interest in school during those years. But I do remember with a fondness a diminutive, bespectacled, white-haired man in his eighties by the name of Mose, who led his charges to the rallying cry of "fight-team-fight" as he stood facing us in the makeshift bleachers on stage during those high school basketball games played in the Recreation Gym.

And those dull end-of-the-year awards programs – dull at least to us non-achievers – were made worthwhile, actually something to look forward to, when the final act in these proceedings brought on stage Homer Fratt, Harold Schumurth, Fred Leist, and Carl Traeger blending their voices as they sang in four-part harmony "The Halls of Ivy."

Everyone who was restless was quiet then, content to listen to a performance by a quartet of three classroom teachers and one vice principal humanizing themselves in their rendition of this grand old song.

Driver Education

The lessons, such as they were, began on a Sunday morning south of town in the middle of Oregon Street road. My instructor, Jim Last, another 16 year old, whose father owned the Brooklyn Diary, a small milk bottling outfit operating out of his garage on Sixth Street tutored me in the fine art of driving in return for helping him on his Sunday morning milk runs that ended up at the Lone Elm cheese factory in the Town of Black Wolf.

The instruction started when we were safely out of town and far away from city traffic, although in the early 1950s, at seven on a Sunday morning, when rural living was still a way of life and the mushrooming of residential boundaries still in its infancy, the chances of meeting another car on the two-to-three mile stretch of road was slim.

Beveled over time and having no shoulders, the middle of this country road seemed the safest place for this apprehensive driver who, when alternating between breaking and exhilarating was, in all fairness, trying to guide the truck along a straight line to the intersection of Nekimi and Oregon's Street roads without running off the road or hitting another car. Forced to listen to the distracting clanging of milk cans sliding back and forth against the pickup's metal sideboards, and the occasional horn blast from a car going in the opposite direction must have given my instructor second thoughts.

It was always a relief to hand the reins over to Jim when I took a right at the town line where the truck was backed-up to the factory's loading dock.

There were other on-the-road experiences provided by this same good friend that helped prepare me and a few others for adult living. Jim owned a '37 Studebaker and liked to take some of his friends, in the dark of the night, to his favorite speeding locale, South Park.

Driving well over the posted speed limits along those winding roads, Jim would purposely tip his car from side to side, careen on two wheels, squeal the tires, narrowly miss trees posing as innocent bystanders while instructing his three passengers just to hang on tight and enjoy "the thrill of your lives."

After multi-sessions of this youthful exuberance, the lug nuts on his back left wheel tore loose one night while driving, pedal to metal, unto Minnesota Street from Fourteenth. As the car tipped on two wheels, nearly overturning, gravel flying, sparks soaring like a July 4th fireworks, the car, what was left of it, finally grounded to a halt.

The two of us seated in the back, not knowing what had transpired, spotted a tire bouncing along the grass terrace on Minnesota Street finally coming to rest under a large elm across the street from the Cellar Tavern.

Some weeks later, thinking I was no longer in need of an experienced co-pilot and wanting additional behind-the-wheel experience, I decided to take my brother's 1929 Chrysler for a spin.

It was in the early evening, as I neared the end of an unauthorized drive, close to the hour of darkness when a cop, walking his beat on North Main Street, shined and wiggled his flashlight in my direction. Thoughts of impending doom tore through me like a bolt of lightening as I slowly pulled over waiting for the cop to cross the street and toss me in jail. One of the passengers in the back seat mentioned, with insight uncommon in our circles, that maybe he wants you to turn on your lights.

It was during the following summer, the summer of my 18th birthday, when I decided to apply for my driver's license. After weeks of carefully studying the state driver's handbook along with question and answer sessions with some who had already passed, I breezed through the written portion of the exam.

Knowing that I needed a car for the road test, preferably one with automatic transmission, Darrel Schmidt, a friend, offered the use of his '49 Buick convertible. The car was longer, sleeker, less austere than what I was used to so I was extra careful driving across the narrow reaches of the Main Street Bridge, the shortest route to the police station. Thinking it would not be in my best interest to back up during the opening moments of this coming-of-age test, I paralleled parked across the street.

So far so good.

When the state examiner and I opened the doors and were comfortably seated in this borrowed white convertible, he instructed me to proceed and take a right on Waugoo, a half block up the street. I made sure the person sitting along side noticed I was using each of the three rearview mirrors before I carefully pulled out of the parking space.

As I slowly negotiated the turn onto Waugoo Street, my right rear tire, not noticing the concrete curbing in front of the Northwestern building, slightly jarred the one seated with the clipboard in his hand. Nothing was said although I noticed he made a check mark on my evaluation sheet.

Not hearing anything to the contrary, I continued along with both hands on the wheel, making sure my hand and arm signals were accurate when making turns.

After a few minutes of driving east the officer told me to make a left turn and head towards Main Street and find a spot to parallel park.

I pulled up to an empty parking space in front of the Majestic Restaurant as instructed, put the car in reverse and slowly began backing up knowing full well this was the litmus test.

The traffic in each direction was heavy as I gently steered my friend's prized possession into that narrow opening without once nicking the vehicle in front or rubbing up against the concrete curbing.

We sat for a few minutes as he wrote comments and made a series of checkmarks. When he finished he told me to drive back to the station.

If there is a God in heaven I thought.

Another milestone was celebrated that night at Arvs, a teenage bar across from Sawyer Field, thanks to this kindly officer and the benevolence of Wayne Handy's 18 year old I.D. card.

Meeting Up With Segregation

I was just not prepared. I should have been. I knew the story of Emmitt Till but that did not seem to stick with me, didn't register deep down. The concept of Civil Rights was not yet a watchword in race relations. So when Uncle Sam called me to active duty in the fall of 1957, I had few clues.

There were divisions in our own city, but the barriers to inclusion were not as rigid as they once were, and the obstructions were religious, ethnic, and economic, not racial.

The Sacred Heart Catholics and the Bohemian Highholder crowd in the Knapp Street area kept to themselves, as they no longer felt it necessary to invade the Lutheran neighborhoods of First English and Peace. And the Nordheim district, the outcasts of the north side, was annexed by the city in the early '50s moving them closer to acceptance.

Oshkosh was an all-white community, a community encompassing immigrant Germans, Russians, Irish and their descendants, and Yankees from the east. It did have the Shadds, a black family, living here for some years, but for reasons unclear, they left in the 1940s. And Nancy Jagodinski, a south sider, a few years younger than me, and a member of First English Lutheran, was another token exception. But it's hard to find others.

So when the army called I experienced a much different world than the one I was accustomed to on the south side of Oshkosh.

I was assigned to Fort Leonard Wood, Missouri. I would later discover Missouri was as racially divided as any southern state. The

Klan, Jim Crow, economic hardships, and lynchings were as much a way of life there as it was in the backwaters of Mississippi.

In the final week of army basic training, I began an education that rarely comes from a book. I was allowed, along with others, to venture off post.

As I boarded the bus for Waynesburg, a small community a few miles from camp, I thought a bottle or two of real beer – not the 3.2 stuff served in PXs – and a greasy hamburger with fried onions and a toasted bun would be a welcome change from mess hall food prepared by hung-over privates. More importantly, I desperately wanted to be among civilians again.

But when I got off the bus I saw, much to my annoyance, an ocean of men, like me, dressed in army dress greens, milling about, alone and in groups, hands in pockets, leaning against buildings, or standing in long lines waiting to get into one of the two restaurants in town. There may have been a few local residents on the street but I don't remember seeing any.

I stayed an hour, maybe two, and then caught the bus back to the post. I didn't have that hamburger or full-body beer I had planned. I didn't do anything other than walking, looking, and thinking.

My clearest memory of that day was the posting of signs fronting most Main Street businesses; signs uniformly stating that Negroes and Coloreds would not be served or admitted. The message, warning actually, stunned me, caught me off guard. I was unaware that such blatant racism existed in our country. I should have known, but I didn't. Growing up in Wisconsin had not prepared me.

Feeling a deep sense of shame, I cut my trip short. I was determined, once I got back to the base, to learn as much as I could on race relations. The Post Library would soon become my best friend.

Some months later, after being assigned permanent party at Leonard Wood, I often caught the bus home. When I did it meant spending time in the St. Louis Greyhound bus terminal.

The terminal was classic Jim Crow. I always felt uneasy there but never in any threatening way. Docility, not bellicosity, was what I saw. The system, for anyone who cared to look, was destroying the spirit and will of a people. The expression on their faces, the gait of their walk, the resignation that ran through their bodies was a cultural shock so overwhelming that I chose to look straight ahead or bury my face in some reading material, afraid if I didn't that I might reveal my true feelings.

I witnessed this racial divide upheld by law before in Waynesville but only in a limited way. To sit in this terminal, as I did on numerous occasions, and see blacks segregated in everything from seating arrangements and toilet facilities, to ticket lines, water fountains, and the small adjoining restaurant, I wondered why this was allowed to happen, why this was still going on nearly 100 years after the Civil War.

I wasn't smart enough to know this was the quiet before the storm. The pent-up anger, especially among the young, was bound to explode.

The 1960s were just around the corner.

Work and other New Experiences

Top photo: Main Street 1920.
Lower photo left: railroad tracks on Ceape Street crossing
Main Street on its way through the tunnel.
Top photo right: Main Street in the 1940s looking west towards
High Street. Athearn Hotel is in the background.
Lower right photo: 300 block on Main Street in the 1950s looking north.

Cherry Camp

It was at the age of 12 when I began to look for outside sources of income. My parents thought it was time for me to begin standing on my own. It helped build character and a sense of worth they said, but also, they neglected to say, freed up the family budget for more important things than handing out movie money.

My working life actually got its start a few years before on a New Year's Eve when I was asked to babysit a child under the tender age of one. When the couple arrived home at four in the morning following eight hours of revelry and too many hours after my very trying time with a crying baby, I was dutifully handed a $1 bill and driven home.

I was determined, when I was old enough, to try some other line of work.

I soon ventured into areas of snow shoveling and delivering papers. The paper route provided more of a steady income than waiting for a heavy snowfall, but folding and delivering this free press in the dead of winter, all 400 for the princely sum of $1.75 was not something I considered doing for an extended period of time.

When I was old enough to do work that promised bigger paydays my parents put school clothes on the list of purchases they would no longer make. So at the age of 14 I signed up for Cherry Camp.

I went for the first time in the summer of 1949. The place was Horseshoe Bay Farms, a few miles south of Egg Harbor in Door County. I got the job by answering an ad in the local newspaper.

So in July when the cherries were ripe, a bus, starting in the Milwaukee area, stopped just north of the Oregon Street Bridge to pick up the seven or eight of us who signed on from Oshkosh. After some hours and multiple stops along the way, the bus finally turned off Highway 57 onto County Trunk G and entered this place I would call home until the Erickson's family cherry orchards were fully picked.

The Ericksons, who owned the property, employed three full-time recreation directors headed up by a man we called "Brownie". The three were hired to provide organized activities after working hours and on weekends and to make sure we had something constructive to do with our free time. Part of the director's job was also motivational; to get us to pick more cherries each day.

It was always a mark of great accomplishment on any given day to be one of the top five pickers in camp. When this happened, we were asked to stand and be recognized. Recognition was also given to the table that averaged the highest number of pails picked, and if you sat at the winning table you were served first, excused first, and exempt from work details for the remainder of the day. This had extraordinary meaning in this highly competitive atmosphere of 60 spirited and determined young men.

We were paid 15 cents for each pail picked with a bonus of 5 cents for staying the entire season. Out of our earnings we paid a daily rate of $1.50 for room and board.

The camp was run like the army. We rose at 5:30 A.M. when one of the pickers, in exchange for room and board, played revelry on a borrowed bugle. If that didn't get our attention, one of the directors would. Breakfast was at 6:00 after beds were made and calisthenics taken.

At 6:45 we loaded ourselves on two open two-and-one-half-ton trucks and were transported to the cherry orchard assigned for that day.

Each morning the two trucks, loaded down with about 60 kids, were forced to negotiate a steep incline as we rounded a bend in the road leading away from the lake. And each morning, chugging up that steep grade with lower gears grinding, we made it. But always just barely.

The lunch of sandwiches, chocolate milk or kool-aid and a cookie tasted good after five hours of picking cherries, dragging and setting up ladders, and being on the lookout for "creamers." Amos, employed as a checker and experienced in spotting trees not picked clean, was usually alerted to these transgressions by those of us who were in a race to work the tree brimming to the top with heavy pickings. Amos then would dutifully send the miscreants back to finish their work.

Initially we picked the tart, sour cherries used mainly for canning and baking. The last of the pickings, where the "big" money was made and the competition heated, was the fabled "Lost Forty", the one's loaded down with those large, dark red, sweet, Bing cherries.

When the work day ended, we were loaded on trucks and taken back to camp. There were the usual complaints along the way of slim pickings or of Amos refusing to punch cards when stems were spotted or when the pail was not full to the top with cherries. But the whining usually gave way once we arrived back at camp.

There was basketball, volleyball, softball, swimming, boating, and table tennis to choose from. If you weren't up to that, one could sit in the lounge area, maybe read or go upstairs and lie on your bunk and wonder if today would be the day your name would be called.

Once or twice a week we watched short films after the evening meal, usually the Laurel and Hardy type flicks. Most of us would hoot and holler when the film alluded even in some remote way to the other gender. And when a good looking woman did appear on screen it usually brought down the house.

On Saturdays we were trucked into Egg Harbor, a nearby community of less than a hundred permanent residents. There was not much to do except walk around, buy a soda, a candy bar, and make life miserable for owners of antique shops by walking into their places of business en masse, touching and not buying. There were no movie houses, bowling alleys, no place to hang out. For all we knew mothers locked their daughters up for the few hours we were there.

A talent show ended the season. The directors and some of the kids would dress up and display their talents in individual and group acts. The show provided laughs, some clean fun, and put us all in a good mood.

The most memorable of these performances occurred during that first summer. A boy from Milwaukee, we called Frenchy, came on stage and sang "Gentle Alouetta." This seemed so out of character for this small, hard-nosed kid, whose language ruffled even the best in our crowd.

Most of us became amused when he appeared on stage and began to sing. We laughed, we jeered, we pointed, and we did those things kids often do to ridicule others. But the room soon became quiet as we listened to this street-smart kid with an authentic French accent and a softness no one thought he had. It was one of the most moving experiences in my yet young life.

I enjoyed the regimen of camp, the competition, the opportunity to make new friends and the challenge of doing something away from home and seeing it through to the end. When we all sang 99 bottles of beer on the wall as the bus headed south towards home that feeling of belonging and being a part of something whole brought me back three more times to this place where cherries were picked and friends made.

Working the Pits

In the fall of 1949 I began work at the T&O Bowling Lanes as a pin boy. None of the other employment opportunities open to a 14 year old offered the deep pockets of ready cash as pin setting did. For the next four years I set up pins and fell in love with the game of bowling.

It was by any stretch tiring work. It was, at first, difficult to keep up with those whose pin setting years numbered more than one. When your assigned lanes fell far behind, preventing the second shift of bowlers from starting on time, Floyd "Ducky" Driessen, the alley manager, did not always understand.

Yet, I looked forward to those nights when we carried our jugs of water and 12 ounce bottles of Pepsi down that narrow walkway leading to our assigned lanes. The challenge of keeping up with those whose experience outnumbered mine, and the affinity, that sense of shared feelings kept me and many of my friends coming back to this place we would soon call our second home.

We were able to bowl free Saturday mornings. This made all the flying pins and broken bottles, the aching backs and sore hands, the weariness felt in school the morning after, even the impatient two-ballers and the slow play of the bar crowd all seem worthwhile.

During the second year of operation, the T&O replaced the old manual or push-down machines with semi-automatic pin setters. Arno Abraham, the owner, in his attempt to reduce costs, cut our pay by two cents a game. The installation of semi-automatic pin setters, he reasoned, allowed pin boys to earn more money "jumping," or setting up two alleys than working the single lane with the manual machine.

If that was not upsetting enough, the following year "Ducky"

Driessen, speaking for the owner, announced at the start of the season that the pay would be reduced another penny.

It was probably bound to happen given Arno's penchant for budget squeezing and "Ducky's" inflexible, hard-line approach, and our belief as pin boys that we were being used, exploited in ways familiar to those struggling in the labor movement.

I no longer remember who took it upon himself or themselves to right this wrong, although "Wiener" Gruhlke, a fellow pin setter, brought up the names of Don Hirte and Carl Bahr, two erstwhile T&O employees. What I do remember was that an organizational meeting was called.

We met in the old high school auditorium on a school day afternoon. An AFL-CIO organizer was scheduled to be the featured speaker. He would be there, we were told, to give advice, to tell us how to organize, how to form a labor union, how to redress our long-held grievances.

There was a large but nervous group of high school age boys at the meeting that day as an effort was being made to organize pin setters throughout the city. Those of us from the T&O were uneasy, "jumpy" might best describe our state of mind. The word was out that "Ducky" found out about the meeting and was coming to break it up.

As the meeting was being called to order someone stationed as a lookout at one of the fourth story windows cried out that "Ducky" was in the parking lot walking in our direction. Rushing to the window to see for ourselves and quickly spotting this man no one wanted to cross, the auditorium soon emptied of T&O pin boys scampering to find an exit leading away from the building and away from Mr. Driessen.

There was no meeting that day, nor to my knowledge was one planned on some future date. Mr. Driessen had accomplished his mission and the unionization of the city's pin boys was put on hold.

The following year, out of a need to make a change, perhaps save face, I along with a few others, switched our allegiance to the Recreation Lanes. Automation had not yet driven a wedge between management and the hired help, and where Bob Putzer, the owner, sang a softer, friendlier, less contentious tune.

The Summer of 1950

The days had their own rhythm and bearing and their own way of working themselves out. We regularly met at someone's house to chart the day until someone's mother would tell us to find something to do outside. This usually led us to the playground a few blocks away.

Two mornings a week we pedaled our bikes across town to North Park to play baseball in the summer league program. We named ourselves the Ready Raiders after the Oshkosh Giant third baseman, Randy Ready. The motley group that Honky Demler and I assembled played hard, but patterning ourselves after this light-hitting and unpolished infielder, we simply couldn't compete against the likes of the Nifty Neffs and the Yandoli Yanks.

Often the crowning joy of those mornings came after the game. Two blocks away on Merritt Street was a grocery store that served cold Royal Crown colas. We would savor the refreshing flavor before once again returning home to figure out how the afternoon might play out.

Those afternoons with nothing else in the works, I'd fetch my tennis ball from the bedroom and muse about life as a baseball player while throwing this once fuzzy ball against the garage or any other any place where I could get a decent bounce or roll before Mother told me to stop.

I had my favorite team and favorite players as did each of my friends. When the St. Louis Cardinals fell behind the Brooklyn Dodgers in the standings, and Stan "The Man" Musial went 0 for 4 in a game that Harry "The Cat" Brecheen lost, it put a damper on the rest of my day.

But when you picked teams like the Cardinals or the Dodgers as many of us did, there was always a tomorrow. Not so with the Chicago Cubs and Pittsburgh Pirates who perennially found themselves fighting to stay out of the National League cellar.

It would then seem strange that the four of us chose to see our first major league game that day in August.

In the summer of 1950 Honky Demler, Bob Bettin, Stu Werdin, and I, not quite 15, traveled to Chicago to watch the Cubs play the Pirates. How I convinced my mother that it would be safe for the four of us to travel on a bus to Chicago with an overnight stay and a city none of us had been to before, is difficult for me to understand, let alone explain.

I do remember telling Mother that Stu, or was it Bob, had an aunt or some close relative living in Chicago and would put us up for the night. That seemed to be a good card to play. I remember pleading relentlessly, telling her that sleeping arrangements were already made and that the other parents had already told theirs sons they could go.

I whined and played on that theme for days, maybe weeks. My mother, worn out, finally gave in.

I don't recall what the other guys told their parents.

So the four of us on that August morning in the summer of 1950 boarded a Greyhound bus in downtown Oshkosh and headed for Chicago and major league baseball. The closest we had ever been to the "Bigs" before was in our living rooms with the dial turned to Burt Wilson and the Cubs on WGN.

The Cubs and Pirates had been battling to stay out of the National League basement the past number of years with little success. That did not seem to bother us. Bettin and Werdin were Hank Sauer fans and Honky unofficially headed the Ralph Kiner fan club in Oshkosh. Although I would miss seeing Stan Musial and Enos Slaughter, I was just thrilled with the prospect of seeing major league baseball for the first time.

We arrived in Chicago and got to Wrigley Field in plenty of time to watch batting practice and identify most of the players on the field. We had seats some 10 rows up from the third base dugout where our view of the field could not have been better.

These were the pre-Ernie Bank Cubs so good seats were plentiful. Hank Sauer, Phil Caveretta, and Bob Rush anchored the team that year. Sauer led the league in strikeouts and was deficient in the field, but was always among the homerun leaders. Caveretta, my favorite Cub, could field and hit but was in the twilight of an outstanding career. Rush was a hard thrower but seldom came up with more wins than losses in any given season.

I don't recall much about the game, who won, who lost, although I do remember it was high scoring. Kiner and Sauer, however, disappointed us by not hitting any round trippers.

After the game we decided the most urgent thing to do was find overnight accomodations. The aunt and uncle story of course was a ruse.

We were looking for something inexpensive and close to the stadium. There was, after all, a ballgame the next day. We chose to walk Clark Street located just outside the front entrance of the ballpark.

We did not walk far before we saw a hotel that looked affordable. I can still see the four of us standing in the lobby of this shabby, worn-out looking building being told by the desk clerk that they would not accept anyone overnight without luggage. Our overnight bags apparently didn't qualify. We tried another down the street that appeared to be in the same general price range but the result was the same.

Although finding overnight accomodations was a concern of ours, I do not recall that we seriously considered taking the bus home that night if we failed to find a room. After all, we bought tickets for the next day's game, and, perhaps of greater consequence, we didn't care to face up to our bald-face lies. Our parents would not have taken this lightly.

So we continued on our way.

We ended up circling the Loop that evening, a sizeable walk from Wrigley Field. After killing some time, we decided to sleep in Grant Park overnight. Even in the summer of 1950, Grant Park was not a place to be in the dark of the night. Our naivete may have been incredulous to a Chicagoan, but to us Grant Park, other than the size, was not much different from North or South Park back home.

It was a beautiful evening in the park by the water. Thousands were enjoying the music as they walked and picnicked. Couples could be seen lying on blankets enjoying the closeness of their bodies, and, like many others, we people-watched as we ate our hotdogs and drank our sodas. Although I had more than a little concern about our talk of sleeping in the park, I was enjoying what this day so far offered.

When the park thinned out and the sun was about to set, we began to think seriously about sleeping arrangements. We rounding up four park benches far enough away from Michigan Avenue so strolling couples and others out on this warm evening would not be able to spot four out-of-town teens lying down on public property.

We placed the benches in a straight line facing Lake Michigan. And much to our credit we did have the presence of mind to make out a rotating schedule of lookouts for the evening ahead. I was to be third on duty. The time of my watch was scheduled for 2:00 A.M.

It wasn't long into my watch when I noticed a man walking back and forth across a walking bridge no more than 50 feet away. He would stop and stare, continue on, and 5 to 10 minutes later, reappear repeating the pattern. It was still early in my shift so I waited, hoping that he would eventually go away. But the intervals became shorter and he got closer and closer.

Frightened by what I perceived as his intentions he disappeared before I could wake the other three. Not being able to see the intruder and displeased that I woke them, they shrugged if off and went back to their sleeping positions. Apparently alarmed, our strange visitor stayed out of sight for the duration of my watch.

Following a short conference after he reappeared on the next person's watch, we decided to leave the park.

We began a slow walk in the direction of Michigan Avenue while trying to come up with a plan that would occupy the hours ahead. It was still nearly eight hours before the Cubs would open Wrigley Field to paying customers. When we were close to exiting the park a policeman in a patrol car spotted us. Stopping along side he asked where we were from and what we were doing in the park this hour of the evening.

We told our story.

I can still see him shaking his head and smiling, not from disbelief, but simply for the incredulity of what he was hearing from four green kids from Oshkosh, Wisconsin. When he regained his composure, he told us that Grant Park was a dangerous place to be at night and that murders were not uncommon there. In fact, he said, one had occurred the previous week. He suggested that we stay at a restaurant until daybreak and pointed to one nearby saying that it would be safe there.

We thanked him and walked those few blocks to this overnight eatery. We ordered hot chocolates after explaining our situation to the waitress on duty. She, being a motherly-type, watched over us as we slowly drank a cup or two of this chocolate drink and read and reread the one newspaper someone had previously discarded.

When daybreak finally came we began the long trek back to Wrigley Field, a jaunt of at least a half-dozen miles.

Game time was still 6 hours away.

After what seemed hours of endless walking, we spotted an old abandoned warehouse within earshot of the ballpark. Tiptoeing inside, we cautiously looked around afraid we might find someone bent on throwing us out or, worse yet, doing us wrong. Finding no one working or lying about, we convinced ourselves better accomodations would not be found.

By late morning this unventilated place became unbearably hot, and concerned that we might be discovered we continued on to the stadium.

We were the first ones in the ballpark that day. That I remember. What I don't remember was who won or whether Kiner and Sauer hit those round trippers we came to see. Nor do I remember much about the rest of the day. I was simply too tired to pay much attention.

Main Street

It was a place well beyond reach during my early years of adolescence. My young world was largely confined to four square blocks of south side real estate. Thoughts of Main Street or any place north of the river never entered the narrow range of my young life.

And then I turned 12.

It was the age of work permits. It was an age when young boys could apply for a paper route. Needing spending money and not wanting to tie up every afternoon after school, I rode my bike north of the river to the office of the Shop-O-Gram, the city's free press, to answer their ad in the local paper.

When an offer of a route on the city's gold coast – Algoma Boulevard – and the responsibility to report to the office each Saturday to collect my route money and listen to any complaints that may have been called in my universe expanded.

This new world of mine now included the old Main Street Bridge.

It was the smell of ink, the roar of one lone press, and the box of 24 candy bars which each of us received at Christmas time that induced me to cross that bridge after school on Thursdays and again on Saturday mornings.

The center of the bridge, unlike the current one that raises when a large boat comes through, swung out from side to side. The fear of falling into this river where currents ran swift increased when I reluctantly yielded to others who were brave enough to stand on that part of the bridge that swung open to river traffic.

And that bridge, constructed in the 19th century, had wooden slats for sidewalks. The slats, which over time had warped, were now largely bent and distorted, and the thumpety-thump-thump of bikes being ridden across the bridge – the roadbed had barely enough room for two motor vehicles – could be heard reverberating a block away.

Main Street Bridge

After folding and bundling 185 of those free circulars I pumped my bike to the corner of Jackson and Algoma to begin the route that took me west beyond Murdock Street, past the old family mansions of the Sawyers and Paines, to a place called the Greenhouse Tap. The bartender at this out-of-the-way tavern, a man who undoubtedly remembered his youth, tipped me a candy bar each time I handed him his copy.

Oshkosh, during the later years of the 19th century, was not the civilized, caring community we know today. Known for its outrageous conduct when lumberjacks and river drivers and others from the northwoods rolled into town, Oshkosh became the butt of jokes throughout the country. These backwoodsmen, thirsting for fun and excitement, were attracted to the pleasures Oshkosh's unscrupulous merchants provided. The customary inhibitions of the times had no claims on those who were determined to engage in the sordidness our Main Street offered.

At these times the good citizens simply stayed away. In their place were these would-be-sinners in their inevitable deep state of inebriation, discovering, after too many rounds, that their money was running out and having not yet stumbled upon the "love of their life," usually found themselves in a barroom brawl or lying face down in the street after enjoying some "playful fun" with the boys.

Over the course of years the city changed but there were still plenty of saloons that lined Main Street and its arteries. They were now tamer, catering to a different clientele. But there were some that provided courage in the bottle and promoted the seamier side of life. And those who were looking for these transgressions, as many who resided here in the '40s and '50s can attest to, sometimes found them in dives like Uncle Buds, The Little Flower, Menzels, and the Deck.

I soon discovered the Downtown Oshkosh was the heart and soul of the city, the hub, the place many chose to celebrate the end of the work week. With its four movie theaters, taverns of every description, restaurants and supper clubs meeting the pocketbook choice of most everyone, Main Street was the center of activity.

For those with discriminating tastes – and there were more than a few – looking for a special place, a place with a touch of class, an air of refinement, a hauteur not altogether uncommon in a city where class distinctions once ran deep, the Athearn Hotel, across from the Opera House on High Street, with its grand history and regal bearing was the choice of most of the city's movers and shakers.

One of my favorite places was the business that occupied the building that abutted the railroad tunnel on Ceape. It was the sporting goods store of Dunham-Fulton.

Al Dunham, the owner, who was kind and thoughtful, pleasant to be around, was also an accomplished bowler and golfer when

The former Revere House (hotel). In the 1940s it was the
home of the Shop-O-Gram.

still in his eighties. His protégé, Killian Spanbauer, who was always helpful, was learning the trade that would soon carry his name.

Just up the street and signaling the time remaining on those late afternoons of working and shopping before the buses arrived to take its riders home for the supper hour was a large standing clock in full view of everyone within a block or two of its keeper, Anger Jewelers. A few doors down was Buehler's Meat Market where Bob Pribbernow, a raconteur of notable skills, plied his trade. Across the street was the Del Rio where I enjoyed my first Main Street tap.

I often stopped at Carmel Crisp, next to the Majestic Restaurant, before taking in a movie at one of the downtown theaters. The Strand was the largest and the one I preferred. It was a grand, ornate palace, comfortable in its slight pretentiousness making even the poorest of movies worth the price of admission.

Strand and Oshkosh Theaters

Of the places to dine or to have a cocktail, the Peaock attracted its share of customers. Sitting at the bar early on a Friday evening, I hummed and sometimes voiced the old favorites effortlessly played on the piano by Kay Brenchley while waiting for my girlfriend to finish work. The evening manhatten and martini, steak and lobster crowd might have chosen to dine at Wussow's, the Roxy or Rusty's Club 375, one of the three Main Street supper clubs.

Rusty Larsen's Club 375, a narrow, smallish place served a martini for a buck and a small tenderloin, potato and salad for two and a quarter. Rusty, always behind the bar, nestling comfortably on a bar stool in the back corner waiting for drink orders from his waitresses when not serving his bar crowd, was a friendly sort and a throwback to former times. He loved to talk about Oshkosh of his and my father's time.

And who after a night on the town did not stop at the Checker Grill across from the Raulf Hotel for a greasy hamburger, an order of fries, and a cup or two of black coffee hoping, as so many did in this crowded diner after the bars closed, to neutralize the alcohol which seemed to have settled in every nook and cranny of the body.

Main Street was also a shopping center with its department stores, five and dime emporiums, and a large number of men's clothiers. The men's fashions began with the Hub and Seese-Hall on the lower end of the price and quality scale and ended upstream with names like the Continental and Spoo and Sons. For women, it was simply a matter of having a preference between two quality stores. Mangels and Christensens, located across the street from each other.

But the department stores of Klines, Sears, J.C. Penney, Montgomery Ward, the Boston Store, and W.T. Grants were the main attractions for downtown shoppers. It was at W.T. Grants where my older brother's girlfriend worked behind the candy counter. When I walked through their revolving door and placed my 15 cents on the glass display case, she, with a wink and a smile doubled the amount of candy a dime and a nickel would ordinarily buy.

In the fall and spring after the school day ended and when the weather was nice and I not in any particular rush to get home, I would wander over to Kresges and Woolworths on Main Street, browse their aisles, check out their specials at the sandwich and soda counter, and, after checking the time, walk to the Boston Store, one half block away, and wait for the bus that would take me home in time for the supper meal.

Main Street in the 1940s

First Date

It was a late, summer-like afternoon in May when my mother, with a solemnity common to mothers sending off their sons on first dates, cautioned me to be thoughtful and caring as this was a special time in every young woman's life.

Nodding my head and saying a few okays and yeahs as I reached in the fridge for my date's corsage, my mother, not wanting to spoil the evening before it began, reminded me, with a smile and a look of concern, to have fun and enjoy the evening.

With that I began a journey into the land of the unfamiliar, the barely explained, feeling uncomfortable and a bit out of place in a suit and tie I was not used to wearing and wondering if I was up to the task.

Wanting to avoid those side-way glances and knowing smiles you often get from adults when carrying a boxed corsage and dressed in your Sunday best, and not wanting to bump into any of my friends asking questions and poking fun, I chose the side streets to walk to this place on the other side of town.

My date greeted me with a smile after I knocked on the front porch screen door, and, after a round of introductions, she asked her mother to pin the corsage. "It matches so well with the dress" I remember each of them saying. Her parents, much like their daughter, were friendly and reassuring and, as we were about to leave, told the two us to enjoy ourselves.

I don't know what they told her before I arrived but I was off to a good start. The Temple, where the Job's Daughter's dance was to be held, was only a block away so the car I did not have wasn't necessary.

As we entered this four-story stone structure, built at the turn of the century, I followed my date to a receiving line commandeered by the Women's Auxiliary of the Free Masons. The formality of all this was new to me. I tried to act that I'd been to these social affairs before, that I was not entirely rooted in south side behavior.

We soon joined some of her friends who had already arrived, and after a round of introductions, a glass or two of refreshments, and some friendly chatter the two of us, along with a few of the others, headed to the dance floor.

It was in a square dance unit in gym class where I last practiced my moves, so I was a little nervous as we stepped to the rhythm of a slow two-step number. The initial awkwardness we both felt soon passed and our movements were no longer marked by caution.

We continued dancing, sat a few out and danced some more. That and eating cookies, drinking punch, the obligatory visiting, and the usual idle chatter found at these evenings was the model the two of us and most others followed.

Although I was trying to be attentive, trying hard to follow my mother's instructions, too often I found my mind wandering in places far removed from this place where formality and manners ruled. Had it not been for my date's quiet laughter, bright smile, and a contagious enthusiasm that lifted my occasional indifference, the evening would have been largely forgotten.

When the dance ended she took the lead orchestrating our goodbyes and thanking the adults who chaperoned and handed out refreshments.

On the walk back to her house, I thanked her for inviting me to the dance and for making the evening enjoyable. As I stood facing her on her front porch, not knowing what else to say, what else to do, I attempted to engage in small talk, but was unable to say anything that made sense. As I nervously shifted from side to side unable to speak, the mounting silence gave way to her saying: "I better go in."

I no longer recall, as we stood there, if the thought of asking for another date occurred. I did consider kissing her but my mother's homily was still buzzing around inside my head, besides no one else cued me in on the propriety of such a move. But then again few knew I was there.

It is at high school reunions where we now see each other. We talk, laugh some, smile, remember. As we do, I think back to my mother and what she said about that day in the life of every young woman and I want to tell her that she was only half right.

Oshkosh Taverns

They were the social centers of Oshkosh, the meeting places in the '40s and '50s. Others might make a case for the churches but in the eyes of those still grubbing for wages and those of us growing into adulthood, it was the tavern.

There were no shortage of taverns in this city of 40,000 - 117 by one count. Most were within walking distance of anyone with a thirst for a taste of barley or simply a need to get out and be with the boys. Though taverns were no longer the sole refuge of the male specie, there were still a few still not willing to address the social changes that free thinkers believed were long overdue.

Utechts, on 6th and Ohio, across the street from the Hour, still carried on the traditions and tastes of the working man's turn-of-the-century saloon. It was a small walk-up where you could belly up to the bar for a shot of booze and a glass of beer. With no bar stools, no seating of any kind, and only one toilet facility, it was no place for the fairer sex, the occasional drinker, or the highball and martini crowd. The real drinkers, the two-fisted ones, who put down 15 cents for a small shooter and the 10 ounce glass, were the ones that made Utechts their second home.

I was 21 when I first entered Utechts. Three of us, the groom and two of his groomsmen, thought we should celebrate the day's coming event by having a shot and beer at this south side institution.

It was shortly after eight when we walked in that morning. The place was already packed, two and three deep at the bar, a few still waiting to be served by the one bartender on duty. They all, as close as I remember, looked like regulars to me, and it was apparent that those who had not yet been served or served fast enough didn't take kindly to the three of us elbowing up to the bar.

After forcing down the brandy and beer with a series of wincing gulps (the other two seemed to enjoy what they were doing) we left. But it was the stares, the looks of disapproval, the feeling of being uninvited that stayed with me the rest of the day. This was their place and they did not take kindly to intruders.

My very first tavern experience came early. At the age of eight my mother sent me two blocks away to Norkofskys on Oregon to tell Dad supper was ready. While waiting for him to finish, the bar owner, not wanting the guilt to spread to the rest of the after-work crowd, handed me a bag of Planter's peanuts to munch on while Dad, still deep in conversation, finished his two bottles of Peoples. His kindness and the sight of Dad enjoying himself in the company of friends planted a seed in me, that I must admit, took root and never lost its bloom.

There was nurturing along the way. Jimmy Pollnow, proprietor of the Acee Deuce Bar and Bowling Alleys, one of the really nice guys in the tavern business, allowed us to play cards, drink pop, and tip an occasional glass of beer in his bar room on Saturday afternoons when we were still in our middle teens. Later on, when we were raising families of our own, we came back to this place on the corner to ask his son Herb to sponsor our teacher softball team.

The National Tavern was our destination on Friday evenings after a night of setting up pins. We walked those two blocks from the Recreation Bowling Lanes to order their perch plate with french fries for 35 cents. Downing a Pepsi or two while taking in the crowd and talking over the day's events was a heady experience. The aroma of fish and hamburgers and onions cooking on the grill, mixed in with the smell of beer and sawdust on the floor gave the place a feeling of belonging, of being part of the wider community of working-class folks. There was never a problem being turned away even at the late hour of eleven as long as we behaved.

There were more than a few taverns, rumor had it, that paid the cops to look the other way. Tad's Bar, Hour Tavern, and LeRoy's

Acee Deuce softball team. Bottom row: Bill Campbell, Dave Morrison,
Jim White, Don Erickson.
Middle row: Tom Wagner, Fred Kubsch, Doyle Hudson, Ron La Point.
Top row: Leon Thompson, Ken Kubeny, Tom Hagen, Louie Mason

Bar were among those south side drinking establishments catering
to the underage crowd. When we entered these places, we entered
them cautiously, understanding that certain behaviors would not be
allowed. So we watched and listened and mostly learned. And soon
we were ordering beer with our food and sometimes just the beer
alone. And I think it worked. It worked because we were in the
world of adults. In a sense we were being chaperoned, our behavior tempered by their presence.

The Hour Tavern, with its booths along the outer walls, a
dance floor in the middle, a jukebox playing the top forty, and a
kitchen serving inexpensive food, was the favorite place of the not-
yet-21 crowd.

The Hour was the place of the overlapping, one-half pound hamburger for a quarter, and a T-bone steak priced at six bits. It was a place to take your date, dance some, get acquainted, and order sloe-gin fizzes and gin bucks. When the beat cop entered the front door, we either ran out one of the two back entrances or quickly drank what evidence remained in our glasses. We were always uneasy when we saw that uniform of blue and white swagger up those steps and enter this south side supper club despite the assurance of the owners, Jerry and Harry Witt.

In the early 1950s, a law legalizing 18 year old beer bars was passed. It didn't take long before Hergerts, Arvs, Ralo, and the Loft opened their doors to this eager but mostly inexperienced crowd.

These were drinking establishments only. No Friday night fish frys here. And with the exception of the people on duty, no adult supervision either. When the adults did come, it was usually the police breaking up fights or arresting someone who had too much to drink.

The young, with alcohol in their veins, were not always able to mute their tendencies to protect, defend, or simply contain their eagerness to fight. Sexual tension and male machismo were the usual culprits. Poor Ma and Pa Hergert, an older couple, who decided to give up the ice cream business and open a beer bar in their own home had to contend with the pushing and shoving, the fist fights, the scattering of stools and chairs when the testosterone levels got too high.

Among other things beer bars served as a central casting place for the unattached. The array of choices was far greater than they were in the neighborhoods many of us clung to. When the owners of places like the Loft and the Rail offered live music a still larger clientele was attracted. Although the under-21 crowd was not an untapped resource for the tavern owners, it had not, before the passage of this law, been fully addressed either.

The time of beer bars and friendly taverns, of adult acceptance and supervision, helped shape those of us who get together each year to rehash those days. We tell our stories that have been told time and again and they still make us laugh. They never get tiresome. They make us feel good about who we are, about that part of our past, about the common thread that ran through our early lives. Then one of us, when the stories start to repeat, offers up a toast.

We talk when we get together like this of such places as Art Noe's Bar, our first softball sponsor; of the Three Oaks and our celebration of victory over Mueller Shell until it was taken away on a technicality; of Punky Nigls and the laughs we had at our many shortcomings and overall ineptness; of LeRoys and our struggle to reach parity with Mueller Shell and Sunlite Dairy, and LeRoy Jungwirth's indifference as long as we continued to laugh at his gentle sarcasm and stop in for drinks after the game; of Haberkorns where we drank beer and played shuffleboard when we didn't care to chase girls after a hard night on the diamond, and; of the Acee Deuce where victory on the field was not the accepted measure of success partially tells the story of our ball playing days.

For those of us who sang, mostly in four-part harmony, at Tony Koeck's Stop and Go accompanied by George Stadler on the accordion, we think of those songs that are rarely sung anymore.

Our attendance at the Club Ohio, the Union Bar, VFW, Columbus Club, and the Eagles at all those uninvited wedding receptions brings a smile to our faces as we think of all the free beer we drank and the crop of girls we looked over. Stories are told but should be mostly forgotten on some of those nights when good sense did not rule.

Most of these places are gone or have taken on new names, a new look. But there are still a few that serve peanuts with your beer and a six pack to go. Occasionally you run into one where they serve, for under three bucks, a hamburger with fried onions on a toasted bun

But it is when I walk into Repp's Bar across the bridge on Oshkosh Avenue I feel once again back home. To see the working and retired crowd bent over the bar drinking beer, a few counting change, one or two kibitzing with the guys at the sheepshead table or with those playing cribbage, a few talking to friends or getting the day's gossip from Denny or Al, and the one or two content in the quietness of their thoughts, makes me think of a time that is now quietly slipping away.

Repp's Bar in the 1950s

Sports and Entertainment

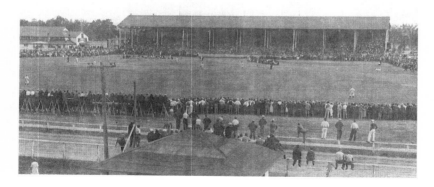

Top photo: All Star fans at the Northwestern Railroad Depot waiting for
their 1942 World Champion Oshkosh All Stars return from Chicago.
Lower photo: 1934 exhibition baseball game between the Chicago Cubs and the
St. Louis Cardinals at the Winnebago County Fairgrounds on Murdock Street.

The City Marble Championship

It was nearing the supper hour on this warm spring day in 1942 when my mother instructed me to go down to the school grounds, one block away, and fetch my two older brothers home for the evening meal. Dad, when he got home from work, liked to sit down and not wait for kids.

So when I spotted them at the far end of the school grounds near the back fire escape, I rushed over and told them supper was ready, that Dad would soon be home from work, that Mom wanted everyone home on time. Rich and Bob, my two older brothers, not wanting to leave, knowing they had a good chance to win the school marble championship, sensed an opportunity to divert my attention from my stated mission by persuading the adult in charge to allow me to enter the tournament.

When the contest ended, well after the supper hour, this first-grader, proudly holding on to his newly acquired first place blue ribbon, matched stride for stride with his two older brothers as we hurried on home to a meal no longer waiting.

On the day of the 1942 city-wide marble championship, my mother unable to chaperone the day of the tournament, instructed my brother Richard to make sure I was on time for the opening round. Rich, who did not place at the Jefferson School shoot-out and was to begin his first year at South Park Junior High in the fall took my hand, like our mother instructed, as we began our journey to Read School and to the promise land.

Thoughts of grandeur raced through my mind as we continued down Ohio Street. Holding tight to my small bag of shooters, the two of us soon approached the Wisconsin Avenue Bridge. On the downside of this concrete arch we could see Algoma Boulevard, the street Mother told us Read Elementary School was on. Thoughts of plying the trade I learned in backyards and in driveways and on the grounds of Jefferson School now made me nervous and apprehensive.

Read School in the early part of the 1900s

When we arrived at this school on the corner of Wisconsin Avenue and Algoma Boulevard there was no one there when we looked around. No one. In that brief moment my heart toppled from my throat where it was momentarily stuck to the pit of a now empty stomach. Thinking we might have arrived early, maybe even gotten the time wrong, we waited. And waited.

The waiting and watching, the looking up and down the street continued for well over an hour. No one came. Rich, seeing the situation hopeless, decided that it was time to leave. I was devastated as we trudged back towards home.

Mother, soon after discovering we were at the wrong school, tried to lift the gloom weighing heavily on her third offspring by promising there would be other times, other years. But the city, we would later find out, and for reasons of its own, chose not to sponsor marble tournaments during the remainder of the war years.

It was 1947, my final year at Jefferson, when a championship format was again started. It was a long wait. I would be at the right place this time. No longer would Lincoln Elementary School be confused with Read. It wasn't much of a challenge winning at Jefferson that year as few entered the tournament. Read School and the City Championship and a lost opportunity were now the only things on my mind.

When I arrived on that Saturday morning six blocks west of the spot the two of us had impatiently waited five years before, I felt prepared, anxious to show what I could do, fully expecting to erase the memory of that not-so-distant past.

But when I looked around I became alarmed. The chalked marble circles were drawn on asphalt, not on dirt as I was used to. When players were instructed not to raise their shooting knuckle off the ground I knew this spelled trouble.

I walked home that day feeling an emptiness I had not felt before. I made it only to the second round, being soundly defeated by someone comfortable with asphalt and not wary of placing his shooting knuckle firmly on the ground.

I knew this would be the end of the road for me and my love affair with marbles. I needed to find something else, something that would restore my sense of self, something that would replace this game peppered with a vocabulary not heard anymore.

The Team

We often talk about this time and I'm not sure why, although the few of us who do cannot seem to get through a conversation without bringing it up. Why we choose to retrieve this part of our past we can't seem to let go, a past that would be quickly dismissed if explored by others, remains a question not easily answered.

Maybe it's the connection we once had with school friends that the intervening years clouded over, a connection once real and satisfying but, as it has done for so many of our adolescent friendships, proved more peripheral than we would have liked.

A few years ago at our high school reunion I was stopped on my way to the bar. A classmate, who I had not been close to for sometime, asked if I had a few minutes to talk. He wanted to know if I remembered the players on this long-ago, almost forgotten softball team he and I played on. He said he remembered a few names but had trouble remembering the others. It was clear, as we continued to chat, that it was important that he know.

After struggling in our attempts to complete the lineup of this long-ago team I promised to get back to him.

His need to know was a longing to rediscover a life journey. He was trying to understand where he had been, who he had known. It wasn't nostalgia at work here, this was something more profound.

There are in most everyone's memory bank remembrances that are special, keepsakes from the past, reminders of who we were, who we are. We are curious to know about ourselves and our friends, and of the circumstances that brought us together.

That we wonder about this particular team, this group of players, not yet teens, brought together for the purpose of competing against a neighboring school, seven blocks to the south, in one home-and-away match that has had a life span stretching across six decades should not be at all surprising. It is part of our nature.

So who were we? Who were the players on this softball team organized and managed by George Hagene, the school custodian at Jefferson Elementary School nearly sixty years ago?

At one corner of this sixth grade infield snaring ground balls was the hard-hitting Dave "Honky" Demler. His throws from third base into the outstretched hands of Dick Jordan, our first baseman, were mostly on the mark. When on occasion they were not, Dick somehow still came up with the ball.

Kenley Steinert and Jim Marshall, our shortstop and second baseman, and the two who helped raise the team's grade point average, anchored the middle of the infield with a presence seldom seen in sixth grade circles. Kenley could backhand a ball going to his right as well as any twelve year-old had the right to do.

Patrolling left field, which often meant standing in the center of Minnesota Street when a power hitter came to bat, was Gerry Brickham, whose peripheral vision allowed him to side-step cars coming in either direction.

In center, left of the large elm that was partially uprooting the concrete sidewalk, was Tom "Teamer" Hansen, who had a knack for snagging fly balls, and coaxing Jim Marshall to play slightly to the first base side of second base. Plying his trade in right field close to the outstretched building housing the kindergarten and to the left of "Teamer," our top ball catcher, was Billy Footit.

Rounding out the squad was the battery of Ron La Point toeing the rubber with his figure-eight style of pitching, and the sure-handed glove of Gerry Stegemeier behind the plate.

We didn't know back then what was waiting for us. We didn't know who we were going to become or what direction our lives would take. We didn't know that everything changes and that life produces its own peculiar flow.

A few still keep in touch and the memories of those days still play a melodious tune when we sit back and reminisce. But a lingering sadness remains. Dick Jordan, suffering from an incurable heart disease, died shortly after that high school reunion and before the roster of this team, which meant so much to him, was fully addressed.

Oshkosh All Stars

They played during a time when two-hand set shots, one-hand push shots, and under-hand free throw shooting was the fashion of the day; when the tallest player might be six foot five or six and a good offensive night might bring 10 or 12 points in the scoring column across from your name.

It was an era when professional basketball was still played in small cities; when the landscape was dotted with franchises across the Midwest, and a period when Oshkosh was known for something other than bib overalls, wood chips, and Saturday night brawls on Main Street. It was the time of our own Oshkosh All Stars and the National Basketball League.

The All Stars debuted in 1929 as an amateur team and eight years later joined the National Basketball League. They played at different city locations until South Park Junior High School on the city's south side was completed in 1940. Two years later, this team, coached and managed by Lonnie Darling and packed with former college stars, brought home a World championship to this city of 40,000. But sadly and unexpectedly the franchise which put Oshkosh, Wisconsin on the national sport's map would be forced to disband some eight years later.

Its undoing was unavoidable. The team's revenue source was tied to an auditorium with a seating capacity of just over 2,000, an arrangement that would, in this growing and soon-to-be lucrative sport, inescapably bring about the end of professional basketball in small cities like Oshkosh.

My love affair with the All Stars started in grade school and continued through junior high. Honky Demler and Teamer Hansen,

Oshkosh All Stars World Champions 1942. From left: Nesbit, Engdahl, Shipp Kominich, Englund, Coach Darling, Edwards, Berry, Prasse, Barley, Riska. Inset: Witasek

two close friends, more than matched my enthusiasm for this team that once took Oshkosh to the heights of the sports world.

That's all the three of us talked about during the school year, other than arguing the merits of the upcoming boxing matches between Rocky Graziano and Tony Zale or Willie Pep and Sandy Saddler or rehashing the National League pennant race.

My usual place was lying close to our Philco radio, pencil in hand over a lined sheet of paper already columned the night the All Stars played. I penciled in the score the night Bob Carpenter of the All Stars scored 40 points, the first to ever reach that number.

But whenever I had a 50 cent piece not already earmarked, I would, with Teamer and the always excitable Honky, purchase a ticket to sit on the make-shift bleachers on stage. Having our view partially blocked by an overhanging backboard didn't diminish the excitement generated by watching our very own professional basketball team.

We mimicked our favorites. Teamer would practice his Floyd Volker one-hand push shots from the left corner during our eighth grade basketball practices. Honky, with his sing-song style of ranting, thought he was the second coming of Leroy "Lefty" Edwards after he lobbed in one of his hook shots. Yours truly, while attempting the flat-footed two-hand set shots of Charlie Shipp, usually drew nothing but air.

The Fort Wayne Zollner Pistons was my favorite team to hate. Bobby McDermott's confident demeanor and patented two-hand set shots and Buddy Jeanette's ball handling had the habit of getting their offense started early. The often dirty play of Jerry Bush, John Pelkington, Blackie Towery, and "Big" Ed Sadowski made it difficult for Lefty Edwards and Gene Englund, our inside guys, to score. When my favorite player was traded to those loathsome Pistons I felt cheated, abandoned. Charlie Shipp belonged in the uniform with white and red stitching.

Edwards, known as Lefty or Cowboy, was the premier player on the All Stars since joining on in 1935. Edwards was voted into the Basketball Hall of Fame in 1971 and was one of two Oshkosh players – the other being Charlie Shipp – on the NBL's all time team. Besides his high scoring average and patented left-hand hook shots, Lefty had a reputation for his defensive "skills."

Sandy Padive in his book, <u>Basketball's</u> <u>Hall</u> <u>of</u> <u>Fame,</u> writes about George Mikan, who he called the first of the great big men. "In 1946, George Mikan signed with the Chicago Gears of the NBL. The Gears were playing the team from Oshkosh, Wisconsin and the Wisconsin team had a center named Cowboy Edwards who was to knock out four of Mikan's teeth."

There were exhibitions played before the start of the regular season and a few were squeezed in during league play. The opponents included the annual appearance of the bearded Michigan House of David and a few colored teams as they were then called.

The Chicago Collegians, a barnstorming colored team, occasionally started off the exhibition season. Nate Clifton and the New York Renaissance, also known as the Rens, and recognized as the premier professional basketball team of the 1930s, would play here now and then as would the Harlem Globetrotters.

The All Stars didn't usually draw well when they came to play. Maybe it was the strangeness of it all, a feeling of discomfort in a city where blackness was confined to its tarred roadways. For some it may have been the perceived inferior play of those who were relegated as second-class citizens even in the sports world.

Jump ball between the All Stars and Pistons at South Park School

In his recently published book <u>On</u> <u>The</u> <u>Shoulders</u> <u>of</u> <u>Giants,</u> Kareem Abdul-Jabbar wrote: "On March 28, 1939, eight young black men from Harlem anxiously stood on the polished wooden floor of the Chicago Coliseum facing eight white men in the final championship game of the first-ever World Professional Basketball Tournament. Surrounding them was a sold-out crowd of three thousand raucous fans – most of them white, most of them shouting out the name of their favorites: the all-white Oshkosh All Stars."

The black team was the New York Rens.

The organizers of the tournament invited what they considered the top twelve teams in basketball. Two of the teams invited were black: the Rens and the Globetrotters. This was the first time white and black teams faced each other for the world title.

The Rens had finished the season with a record of 112 wins against 7 losses. Although the All Stars had defeated them the past

7 out of 10 games the teams played, Oshkosh fell in the championship game by the score of 34 to 25.

Three years later 4,000 All Star fans waited at the railroad depot on Broad Street to greet their World Champion Oshkosh All Stars.

And then it all came to an end.

In 1949 the National Basketball Association gobbled up most of the valuable NBL franchises: the Rochester Royals, the Minneapolis Lakers, the Fort Wayne Zollner Pistons, the Syracuse Nationals. Even the Redskins of Sheboygan gained admittance. Oshkosh, with its limited seating, was not invited.

No longer would the Rookie of the Year Dolph Schayes of the Nationals or the scoring tandem of George Mikan and Jim Pollard of the Lakers ply their trade in a gymnasium a few blocks removed from the center of our universe. Bob Davies, Al Cervi, and Red Holtzman of the Royals, Bobby McDermott of the Pistons, Frank Brian of the Anderson Packers, Mel Riebe of the Cleveland Transfers, and Eddie Dancker of the Redskins would also be among those missing. They would now compete in the league that featured "Jumping" Joe Fuchs of the Philadelphia Warriors, and "Easy" Ed McCauley of the Boston Celtics.

A few of the All Stars would sign on with the Oshkosh Stars, a semi-pro team organized later that year in the newly formed Wisconsin State Basketball League. A few retired, others played locally or were picked up by the NBA.

But it soon became painfully clear that the Oshkosh Stars, led by local favorites Charlie and Eddie Erban, and former All Stars Bill McDonald, Gene Berce, Billy Reed, and Bob Mulvihill with occasional help from an old and tired Edwards and a semi-retired Gene Englund would never replace Lonnie Darling's World Champion Oshkosh All Stars, a team led by a left-hand hook shot artist Hall of Fame coach, Adolph Rupp of Kentucky, would later call the greatest player he ever coached.

Sawyer Field

We pumped our bikes in the early summer evenings to the west side where baseball was played. The four of us who regularly made the trip hoped to save the price of admission by climbing the 10 foot cyclone fence on the first base side.

When that failed, as it often did, no thanks to an alert Vic Schinski, the guardian of the gate, we frequently chose to chase foul balls in the parking lot or across the street on Sawyer. The 10 cents not spent could be used on the way home at the Hi-Holder Restaurant.

There were times, however, when the Peters' boys were snagging all the foul balls as they dove and slid between and underneath cars on the gravel parking lot, or when the cheers coming from inside the park were especially loud that we decided to part with our dimes instead of waiting for the seventh inning stretch when the gates opened to all comers.

The place was the Oshkosh Municipal Ball Park, better known to us south siders as Sawyer Field. It was the home of the Oshkosh Giants and a member of the old Wisconsin State League, Class D affiliation, the lowest rung on that slow and arduous climb to the major leagues. The Oshkosh team became known as the Giants when they affiliated with the parent New York club after World War II. Previous to that they had an agreement with the Boston Braves.

But the Braves were not the first professional baseball team in the city. Oshkosh dates professional baseball back to the 1880s when the playing field was located at the old County Fairgrounds on Murdock Street. One of its best players was William Hoy from Ohio. He was known as "Dummy" Hoy throughout his baseball career which, incidentally, lasted 14 years in the major leagues.

Oshkosh's first professional baseball team. Hoy is standing top left

In his book <u>Triumph</u> <u>and</u> <u>Tragedy</u> in <u>Mudville</u>, Stephen Jay Gould wrote about William "Dummy" Hoy. "He played 1798 games nearly all as a center fielder in fourteen seasons and compiled an excellent lifetime batting average of .288. But his greatest skills lay in three other areas: his speed and superior baserunning abilities (598 lifetime steals); his acknowledged intelligence and savvy understanding of the game's subtleties, and; his excellent fielding, particularly his rifle arm. Hoy in a single game in 1898 threw three players out at home plate from his center fielder's position."

Hoy though, as fate would have it, was unable to hear the cheers from the fans in the grandstand. Hoy, who was stone deaf, thus the name "Dummy." was instrumental in getting umpires to change from voice to hand signals when calling plays.

There were others who played professional ball in Oshkosh who made it to the "Big Show". Best known was Hank Bauer, a left fielder for the New York Yankees, who played on those Casey Stengel championship teams of the 1940s and 1950s.

Later on Stan Jok, a hard-hitting third baseman, and a southpaw pitcher by the name of Joe Margeroni played for the New York Giants. Tom Acker, throwing from the right side and the most successful of the three, pitched a number of years for the Cincinnati Reds.

Two of my favorites were Sam Brewer, a Cherokee Indian from Stillwell, Oklahoma, and Tom Gatto, a left hander with exceptional talent. Brewer, the ace of the staff, won over 20 games in 1947, and Gatto, with his big kick and long arms set league strikeout records on three separate occasions.

Neither one made it to the majors. Gatto was killed in an auto accident shortly into his career, and Brewer, despite his promise, never made it beyond Triple A ball with the Minneapolis Millers.

Sawyer Field

There are other names easily recalled. Local players such as Dick Bixby, Swede Erickson, Bob Roth, Lenny Heinbigner, Paul Moylan, and Bob Koss come to mind, as well as young men from the east with names not often heard in this part of the country: Rudy Yandoli, Pete Brozovich, and Joe Battaglia.

And then there was Randy Ready, a third baseman, whose undistinguished two years in Oshkosh was matched by our forgettable performances as his namesake, the Ready Raiders, while playing baseball at North Park in the summer baseball program.

When the ball game ended and our bikes were retrieved, we headed for that place on the corner of Fifth and Knapp, named after the district with Sacred Heart as its centerpiece, and made the decision that was not always easy to come by: whether to buy the two-for-15 cent hot dogs or the 10 cent hamburger.

The Hi-Holder Restaurant as it looked in the early 1950s

Billy Hoeft

Images of that warm April afternoon keep coming back: the scattering of baseball fans lining the foul lines, some with lawn chairs, others standing, anticipating the opening of the 1950 high school baseball season; a few major league scouts on hand waiting to evaluate this tall, slender southpaw everyone came to watch; the mowing-down of batters inning after inning by this high school senior with a fastball unequaled in these parts; the foul ball hit late in the game just beyond the reach of the out-stretched hands of the first baseman; the watchful eyes of those in attendance as they waited for this lanky lefthander to strike out the last batter in the ninth and imprint his name and this city in the annals of sport history.

They are all there.

I rode my bike across town that day to watch this player everyone was talking about. Oshkosh High was scheduled to play a team that had won the Little Ten Conference in the southern part of the state for the past five years. So it was promoted as a test for this 17 year old.

It was no secret that Hal Beatty's Hartford High School team expected a tough game. They and most everyone else associated with high school baseball knew Billy Hoeft was destined for great things. He had already pitched three years of high school ball and had gained a reputation throughout the state. So when the game ended with the Hartford team hitless, it did not come as a great surprise.

"Bill Hoeft declared after hurling his fantastic game" wrote Al Madden in his <u>Northwestern</u> sports column, "that he wasn't working too hard. Bill used straight stuff mostly, but tossed in some curves to left-handed victims. Late in the game Bill uncorked some drops. When Bill became aware of his historic feat he did throw hard he admitted. It was his fourth no-hit, no-run game."

But this game witnessed by a hundred or so lucky fans was not simply another no-hitter. It was much more. This lanky portsider, this 17 year old, who was being watched by scouts from most every Major League team since his sophomore year, made baseball history by fanning 27 straight batters. TWENTY-SEVEN IN A ROW. Not one batter for the opposing team hit a fair ball. According to the scorer, no more than ten to twelve balls were fouled off.

"Not many know to what pains Coach Schneider has gone in grooming the ace lefthander" mused Madden a few days later. "He ate just certain foods and always was sent away from the table with a slight hungry feeling. Then following his game, Bill would get a diathermy treatment for his arm."

But it wasn't merely a diet plan and heat treatments that brought about the success Hoeft enjoyed on the playing field. It was this complement, the blending of a talented athlete and a dedicated coach, practicing the tools of the trade on and off the playing field during his four years of high school that honed his skills and brought him to the level he was currently playing.

Hoeft pitched 5 more games that season. His pitching record his senior year was 6 wins, 0 losses, 72 strikeouts, 8 walks, 9 hits, 3 runs in 52 innings of work.

Madden in his June 5th column noted: "Bill Hoeft, the most sought after prep pitcher in the country, climaxed his brilliant career with a one hit, six to nothing win over Manitowoc. . . Saturday's game wrote finis to the coaching career of Schneider about whom Branch Rickey Jr. of the Brooklyn Dodgers said: 'Much credit must go to Coach Schneider for developing one of the best high school baseball teams I have ever seen."

The Indians of Oshkosh High did not compete in the state tournament that year despite defeating the eventual state champion Menasha High 9 to 0 when they met earlier in the season. According to Madden in his June 9th column: "Big hearted, they (Oshkosh) stood by (by request) and let the smaller and weaker teams battle for the crown."

Just how good was this left hander from the east side who

amassed a record of 34 straight wins until losing one in the state tournament in his junior year. Jimmie Hole, a scout for Oakland of the Pacific Coast League, said that Hoeft was the best he ever saw.

For the next few weeks the <u>Northwestern</u> carried stories of Major League teams eagerly waiting the day of Hoeft's graduation. Unlike today when high school players sign for bonuses in the millions, the baseball rules of the time stated that if a player signed for a bonus – more than $6,000 – he must move up to the parent club after just one year of minor league seasoning.

On June 22, 1950 Billy Hoeft chose the Detroit Tigers over his favorite boyhood team, the Chicago Cubs. The headline and photo of Hoeft signing a baseball contract that day was on the front page of the <u>Oshkosh</u> <u>Daily</u> <u>Northwestern.</u>

The two column story read in part: "Bill Hoeft today signed a one-year contract with the Toledo Mudhens of the American Association – a Triple A club owned by the Detroit Tigers. . . Bill said that he selected the Detroit organization because 'I like that ball club and I know they will treat me the way I want to be treated.' He decided not to sign as a bonus player, but instead chose to sign for a dollar less than the maximum $6,000."

Billy Hoeft never carved out the career many expected him to accomplish. But if his Major League stay of 15 years was not a stellar one it was by most measuring sticks a good one. He won 20 games one year and 16 in another. In the 1960s when he was no longer a starting pitcher he was first traded to San Francisco Giants and then to the Milwaukee Braves.

But it's not his years in the majors that come to mind when I think back some 50 years. No. It's not that. What I think of during the warm days of spring baseball is that late afternoon in April when diamond history was made.

Boxing

There was a time in my youth when the sport of boxing was fashionable; when boys and young men could demonstrate their mettle, their gamesmanship, the strength of their character; when putting on gloves was considered a rite of passage, an act of manliness, a way of measuring up. And when the occasional contentious confrontation erupted into a fight 16 ounce boxing gloves were used to settle the differences.

But boxing was not solely consigned to the young or to those trying to settle a score. Boxing in the '40s and '50s was a national sport, not something relegated to the back page of the sport's page.

Radio first aroused my interest in the fight game. The event was the long-awaited and much publicized heavyweight championship fight in 1946 between Joe Louis and Billy Conn.

Caught up in the hype and hoping Conn wouldn't make the same mistake twice, I listened, as I laid close to the speakers of our Philco console, to this long sought-after rematch with an intensity not uncommon in my small circle of friends. When Louis easily disposed of Conn in the eighth round it didn't discourage me from listening to most every heavyweight title fight featuring names like Joe Louis, Jersey Joe Walcott, Rocky Marciano, and Ezzard Charles.

But it was more than just the heavyweight division that excited me. It was the knockdown fights between middleweights Tony Zale and Rocky Graziano, and featherweights Willie Pep and Sandy Saddler. It was Sugar Ray Robinson's bouts with Jake LaMotta, with the bolo punching style of Kid Gavilan, and the toughness of the Italian from upstate New York, Carman Basilio.

Amateur boxing was also in its heyday. Colleges and high schools featured boxing as a major sport. "Zip" Schuster, a former prize fighter and a non-teaching employee in the Oshkosh school system was the defacto trainer and manager of our high school's boxing program. It was a program as popular in the 1940s as high school basketball and football are today. That it soon disappeared from the activity handbook should not diminish its importance to those who participated and to the many who watched and cheered. Dual matches with area high schools drew large, cheering crowds in the old high school gym. When boxers from Little Chute, Kaukauna, and Shiocton appeared on the card –schools with strong boxing programs – it was standing-room only.

But the loudest and most vociferous crowd was in the afternoons when early dismissal drew a large army of students flocking to the gym to cheer on their favorites in the intra-squad matches that would determine the school's representative in each weight class. But sadly and precipitously, high school boxing programs soon ended.

The death knell to high school and collegiate boxing occurred in a match at the University of Wisconsin in 1950. An unfortunate incident, an unexpected injurious blow, took the life of a promising young man.

CYO matches at St. Vincent's parish still packed them in and the local Boy's Club continued to prepare young men for the Golden Gloves. But that was the extent of boxing in the city in the '50s. And soon even that petered out. Even on the national level the fight game wavered. And then, as it sometimes happens, a revival of the sport was in the making.

The Gillette Razor Company, wanting to hawk its new blue blades to a larger audience, partnered with television to give us Friday Night fights, a program that would soon be as popular as Monday Night football a decade or two later. The savior, the plum in the pudding, was a 17 year old by the name of Floyd Patterson, a soft-spoken, well-mannered young man with a peek-a-boo stance, and a flurry of punches that dazzled and captivated the viewers. The standing-room-only crowd that gathered at Harold's Bar, a little before nine on Friday nights, watched this young man of humble origins climb the heavyweight ladder with each successive win.

Protecting his face as he crouched, elbows close to the body, jabbing and blocking while looking for an opening, then rushing in with his now familiar blitzkrieg of punches brought cheers from this bar room crowd. His bout against the flailing arms and onrushing punches of Thomas "Hurricane" Jackson caused a frenzied excitement not previously seen in this Oregon Street tavern where the drinks flowed and the smoke of burning cigarettes crowded the air.

There were other fights, but the magic of his fists and the charm of his personality that gripped so many of us disappeared too soon. His humbling defeats at the hands of Ingemar Johannsen, later Sonny Liston and Ali saw to that.

But this meek and unassuming young man, a former Golden Glover and Olympic Champ, crouching in that inimitable style of his caught the imagination and fancy of the boxing world when the sport most needed it.

Wednesday Night at the Recreation Lanes

It doesn't look like much from the front as you pass on your way north to the bridge, but then it never did. What it did was house eight of the highest scoring bowling alleys this side of Milwaukee.

Owned at one time by a card-playing foursome of Bob Putzer, "JoJo" and "Porky" Penzenstadler, and Clarence "Gabby" Wirtz, this place with built-in gallery seats and limited parking drew a large, eager gathering each Wednesday evening to watch the Recreation Classic League bowl.

The most closely watched on those nights when standing room was at a premium was Bireleys, a team that held the state record for a three game series. The record would last enough years to swell the pride of the Oshkosh bowling community.

This team, with four of the first five members in the local Hall of Fame, included Matt Muza, Arnie Zuehlke, Bob Putzer, Vic Boeder, and Rudy Nigl.

The lanes admittedly were easy, "grooved" as the saying went. The coating was shellac, a thicker, more durable dressing than that used today. The line to the pocket was steady and sure and even those whose release was in question seemed to easily hook the ball into the pocket.

But it wasn't just the lane conditions which generated scores well above the norm. It was also the pins. They were, the argument went, lighter and dryer, rounder on the bottom. Tipsy was the word often used.

But it would be irresponsible, certainly uncaring not to give due to this place where the lanes looked warped to the naked eye. This was a time before urethane and resin and other technologies that would revolutionize the game. Hard rubber bowling balls with the middle two fingers buried to the second knuckle was the choice of most. Connie Schwoegler's finger-tip grip and Pete Kowalski's EZ Lift were on the market but were not yet widely used.

Most of the city's best keglers were here when the inside of this small, elongated box-like structure was clouded over with the floating vapor of burning cigarettes and cigars. Hub Hielsberg, Eddie Luther, even the up-and-coming "Hezzy" Munsch, who was showing off his talents as an 18 year old in exhibitions with visiting ABC Hall of Famers June McMahon and Andy Varipapa, and being touted as Oshkosh's great young talent for the big time, might run seven or eight strikes in a row. And any number of bowlers, a group including "Shorty" LaFond, Augie Fiebig, "Doc" Russell, "Cully" Genal, Paul Priebe, Eddie Otto, "Buster" Thill, and the Penzenstadler brothers might hit that magical 700 series.

But most eyes were on this team with an orange soft drink emblazoned on their shirts and a state record next to their name.

Matt Muza, with his unmistakable gait and the always-present cigar clenched securely between his teeth, was the bowler Bireleys wanted on top. His steadiness – tenaciousness some would call it – and his short down-and-in hook proved to be the perfect formula for a lead-off man on this team stacked with high average bowlers.

Arnie Zuehlke, the top bowler in the city and one of the best in the state, had a shuffling four-step delivery and a big round-house hook that when started a board or two outside the second arrow drove the pins to the sideboards with a velocity matched only by Dick Zellmer's unorthodox style and sharp-breaking hook.

Bob Putzer with his running start and high release was the middle man on this team. He was one of the first in the city to roll a perfect game, a time very much unlike today when 300s were rare. Traveling almost as fast as the speed of light, his ball splattered the pins more than pushing them back or scattering them from side to side.

Vic Boeder with his left arm flung out as a counterbalance to

Harold "Hezzy" Munsch Jr. Beats
Junie McMahon in Pin Exhibition

Youthful Kegler Wins
Opening Game; Nigl,
Zuelke Fall Before Ace

his low-to-the-ground approach was effective in clearing the alley of pins. Always around the pocket while throwing a semi-roller – a spinner we called it – he usually found himself near the top of the average sheet due to his accuracy and his competitiveness. This competitiveness and a durability few seem to have can, at least in part, be measured by his recent 50th trip to the American Bowling Congress's annual tournament.

But the anchorman was the crown jewel of this team that had

no equals in the city; a city that would eventually make its mark on the national bowling scene.

Although past his prime, Rudy Nigl, with his lit cigar snuggled between his first two fingers on his left hand, was beauty in motion as he glided down the approach stroking the ball into the pocket. He had the smoothest and easiest delivery this side of Connie Schowegler and Ned Day.

When the show was over and high scores announced I took

The Bireley's championship team of 1954-55. From the left is Arnie Zuehlke, Vic Boeder, Rudy Nigl, sponsor Dick Binder, Jim Kosup, Bob Putzer. Kosup replaced Matt Muza who died the previous summer

that long walk home to that place on the other side of Oregon Street dreaming of the day I would wear the blue shirt with the orange soft drink emblazoned on the back.

The Day Fast Pitch Changed in Oshkosh

It happened more than 50 years ago when the city of Oshkosh hosted its Third Annual Optimist Club Central Wisconsin Softball Tournament at the city's new North Side Lighted Diamond.

Coverage in the <u>Oshkosh</u> <u>Daily</u> <u>Northwestern</u> promoted the occasion as a can't–miss event for area softball fans. It would, the paper said "bring together in competition the best teams in this part of the state" including Eddie's Lakeview Club of Racine, a team claiming two of the state's best pitchers.

Oshkosh fielded her own. Throwing in a figure-eight style popularized years before, Rudy Meyer, George and "Ace" Bonnach, John Plier, Johnny Reamer, and Del Voight baffled hitters with an assortment of pitches and were ready for the competition the tournament was expected to bring.

In the northern reaches of the Valley, Bob Diener, Bud Werner, Norm McIntyre, Bob Skally, and Red Cochran had demonstrated their effectiveness as first rate figure-eight hurlers of this tightly wound 12 inch ball. They were ready as well!

There were a few wind-mill types. Les "Cannonball" Dietzen of Kaukauna and George "Doc" Meyer of Oshkosh come to mind. But most who pitched in one of the state's hotbeds of fast pitch softball threw with a bent-knee, swinging of the arm in a wide arc, underhanded motion, building up momentum as the hips pivoted and the body turned.

It was warm and sunny that Fourth of July weekend in 1954 as local fast pitch enthusiasts were about to bear witness to a game that would forever change the face of Oshkosh softball.

It was on the tournament's second day when Eddie's Lakeview was scheduled to play. Warming up on the sidelines, throwing without apparent effort, but with a velocity not seen in these parts before, Jim Chambers and George Lorentzen became the focus of attention. It was clear to most anyone watching that the game's outcome had already played out.

Chambers and Lorentzen simply overpowered the hitters. Pitching in what most considered a side-arm delivery, elbow away from the body, like a hard under-hand throw from the shortstop deep in the pocket – a slingshot deliver it was called, whiplash others might say.

The batters were not ready, having never seen this type of pitching before. Intimidated when stepping in the box, the batter often bailed out before the pitch was released, fearful of being struck by a ball traveling at a speed approaching 100 miles an hour.

I watched these two mow down batters without breaking a sweat and knew the game was passing me by, and, by extension, the game I knew and played was becoming obsolete.

When the weekend was over, Eddie's Lakeview Club laid claim to the first place trophy. Chambers and Lorentzen, pitching in each of the tournament games, had four wins. Three were no-hitters, the other being a one-hitter. The two struck out 77 of the 90 batters they faced.

It would be a few years later when softball communities in central and northern Wisconsin responded. In Oshkosh the experience of the tournament spawned pitchers such as Denny Neitzel, Tom Boettcher, Dick Walgren, Bill Bollom, and Mike Miller. Mueller Shell and Sunlites, two perennial top teams in the city, whose pitching was now considered unsuitably old-fashioned, were soon replaced by Wertsch Motors, Oregon Clothing, and Tommy's Bar, teams that would in the 1960s and '70s compete on the state and national levels with a good deal of success.

But the good old days of a pleasing, mostly harmonious arrangement among the various components of the game gradually faded away. Pitching dominated and interest waned. Frustrated batters, longing for the days of yore, turned to a game popularized in the far reaches of eastern and southern Wisconsin to show case their talents.

Fast pitch softball sadly gave way to a game called slow pitch and an era ended.

Radio

Our family moved into a four bedroom house on Minnesota Street in October of 1944. It was located much to the satisfaction of Dad, less-so Mother, two doors down from the Cellar Tavern. The house commanded a close-up view of the clock tower of St. Vincent's Church and its tower bell tolled every 15 minutes which served as our alarm clock on school days, and a call to get home on time for the supper meal.

Radio was the centerpiece of our family life. Crowned with a white doily and some knick-knacks, and resting close to the comfort of our three cushioned davenport and coal-burning stove, the Philco radio, more furniture than appliance, was our family's prized possession.

Edgar Bergen and Charlie McCarthy, Fibber McGee and Molly, and Jack Benny were favorites of my parents, as were Burns and Allen, and the Great Gildersleeve. Gang Busters, Jack Armstrong, the All-American boy, and the broadcasts of the Oshkosh All Star games were among those I turned to with a degree of regularity.

Although I didn't tell my friends, I often rushed home from school to listen to Billy the Brownie reading those Christmas wishlist letters sent in by second, third, and fourth graders promising to leave cookies and milk for Santa and the reindeer. After giving the low-down on the status of Santa, Mrs. Claus and their helpers at the North Pole, Billy reminded his young listeners to be good little boys and girls. I was still turning that dial to 620 in eighth grade with a regularity difficult to relate to others my age who were beginning to tune-in to the distaff side of life.

And I liked Henry Aldrich during those late afternoons. "Hen-reeeeee! Heeeeeen-re Aldrich! Coming Mother" was the opening line in each of his program installments and is as recognizable as Fibber McGee and Molly's closet in radio lore.

It was easy to like Henry. He was credible to adolescents and young teenagers. He was like us, in that awkward age, ungainly, lacking in grace, making mistakes. He was trying to figure out his place in this new world of his like we were. His teachers and parents fussed over him just as we wanted them to gently push us in the right direction.

And then it all changed.

It was in the summer of 1948 or 1949

Norm Schein, the summer playground director at Jefferson School, invited a few us who were playing on the grounds that day to his house across the street on Tenth to view live television. I thought of my Uncle Louie as we began walking, recalling what he had said to a roomful of adults in our living room on a Sunday afternoon some years before: "Pretty soon we're going to see moving pictures right in our living room. You wait and see."

What we saw were flickering spots on the screen. TV snow it would later be called. Mr. Schein, with his enthusiasm still not in reverse, was trying to pick up WTMJ from Milwaukee. After what seemed as multiple sessions of rabbit ear adjustment we finally made out a man's outline, and then quickly even that disappeared.

I wondered later, after we all left, what all the excitement was about.

The Movies

There were two movie theaters on the south side of town, and for 10 or 15 cents for four full hours of entertainment one could view, free of commercials and that deafening all-around sound, a double feature, cartoons, coming attractions, and a newsreel.

The Mode, on the corner of 12th and Oregon, was the theater of choice when you wanted to be drawn into the story, to be caught up in the action, the suspense. Walking that one short block to the quietness of this theater was a way of shutting out the outside world for an entire afternoon.

The Star, across the street from the Mode, was the most fun for kids. It was not as strictly supervised as the Mode. If you were in the mood to watch a World War II flick or something else that had depth slightly below the surface you chose the Mode. They didn't permit mischief-making there. But if you wanted to have fun and act like a kid, throw popcorn or jujus at someone two rows down you went to the Star. And the Star showed serials.

The serials (we called them chapters) relied on a much-tested device for keeping suspense alive one weekend to the next. It was drama by installments. They were motion picture cliffhangers even in the literal sense.

How many times did the stagecoach plunge over the cliff just as the episode ended? How many times did the wagon laden with burning hay crash into the ranch house killing the besieged hero, his girl companion, and his faithful saddlemate? We knew the hero and those with him had escaped unharmed ready for the next episodic adventure. But the nagging thought that maybe this time they might not escape, tugged at and returned us to the Star the next Sunday, and the next, and the Sunday after that.

Opening night at the Mode Theater

The Star Theater

The Star featured western films of the B variety. The plots, thin as they were, were pretty much alike. There was the ubiquitous cowtown and the barroom brawl, cattle stampedes and the cattle baron, desperados and the deputized men, and always the pretty girl and the reluctant hero. Filling that role were the likes of Wild Bill Elliot, Lash La Rue, Hopalong Cassidy, and the singing cowboys, Roy Rogers and Gene Autry

The images of the hero and his sidekick riding their horses alone or with their band of deputized men, chasing bandits, firing their guns and dodging bullets, getting the outlaws in the end, then riding off into the sunset are there to be retrieved in all of us who spent those countless afternoons at the Star.

But there were downsides to this small box-like theater beyond the insidious noise and rowdyness when you actually got caught up in the plot. Its toilet facilities were in the basement, a dark, dank place. Rumor persisted that rats roamed freely there so one either held it, or, if that was not possible, not take long doing what you had to do.

Then there was Charlie, a little boy in a man-size body who was a fixture on those Sunday afternoons. Charlie had difficulty distinguishing between make-believe and reality. When he became immersed in the film, which was often, he would cry out, shout for the evil-doers to stop, bawl when a dog was run over by a stagecoach, cheer when Hoppy corralled the horse thieves, or when Wild Bill out-dueled the town bully, and clap loudly when the hero and his lady friend rode off into the sunset.

It was a scene beyond belief to those of us too young to understand.

So we were mean, real mean as kids can often be. Charlie frequently went home crying not because of the roller coaster of emotions he experienced. No, it wasn't that. Sad to say, it was because of us; what we said, what we did.

I spent many years watching second-run movies on the south side of town. The theaters were closer and cheaper, and Beernstsens, where penny and nickel candy was sold, stood just across the street.

Wedding Dances

When it began is no longer clear. Perhaps it got started by someone in our crowd reading or overhearing of a Saturday night wedding reception where free beer, sandwiches, and available girls could be found. The excitement of "tipping one back" and walking a girl home and "making out" brought about an eagerness for us to begin plotting strategies that might work.

In our early attempts to enter these Gardens of Eden we were, as you many have guessed, systematically turned back, but despite these fruitless first efforts we continued to plot and scheme, and, with a bit of inventiveness and some moxie, we soon turned it around.

There were plenty of clubs and halls to choose from in this hard-working factory town. Places like the Eagles, Union Hall, VFW, Columbus Club, Westward Ho, Acee Deuce, the American Legion, and the Club Ohio were there for the taking.

We had our favorites. The Eagles and the Club Ohio were close to topping that list, but they were hard to crack. Without a printed invitation or a friendly "guardian of the gate" we relied on what little ingenuity we possessed.

The Club Ohio was a south side hot spot. With its large bar area and its weekend dance bands, its homey atmosphere, and its working man's prices, this place on the corner of Sixth and Ohio attracted the young and old alike.

There were more than a few of us with designs on getting past the uniformed cop on duty hired to ride herd on the flow of interlopers trying to freeload in the upstairs reception area. This was not, needless to say, an easy assignment. There was only one entrance and the stairs – the one we walked up and were frequently sent down – was narrow. Our strategy, when the guardian of this lone entrance was taking his duty seriously, was to mill about in the downstairs bar looking for the right opportunity to present itself. Occasionally we persuaded some invited guest to allow us to tag along.

We were caught more often than not but the sport of it and that chance to meet that certain someone brought us back again, and again.

The Veterans of Foreign War's building alongside Witzke's Tavern on Seventeenth near Oregon Street is still there. They still cater to receptions and provide a friendly place to have a beer and sometimes listen to the guy at the piano with a cigarette dangling and a Captain Andy cap nestled affectionately on top of his head playing and singing those tunes seldom heard anymore.

It's still a place with cash lying on the bar waiting to be spent for drinks with 1980 prices; watch the smoke curl up to the pressed tin ceiling than hang around in a perpetual haze; have a visit that is casual and friendly, and listen to folks uttering gossip and chatter you would expect from sons and daughters of blue collar workers of an earlier Oshkosh.

But as friendly and inviting as this place is today, the VFW was not easy for us to get past those who guarded their two entrances. So we often chose the path that resisted the least when Saturday nights rolled around. That path usually took us north of the river.

There were two places on the northeast side of Oshkosh that were almost next door to each other and this alone drew us there many Saturday nights. Of the two, Union Hall was the one tried first.

The hall stood above the Union Bar in a room designed to host union meetings so its size was suitable only for small receptions. But that did not discourage us. Although it was another upstairs entrance closely monitored we sometimes got through, and when we did, I suspect the monitor on duty, with his knowing smile, was thinking back to those years of his youth.

The Eagles was the grand prize of them all. It was around the corner on Washington Avenue with 12 bowling lanes downstairs, a large ballroom, a bar and a gathering place on the ground level, and a large wrap-around mezzanine section – a perfect place to drink seven ounce bottles of Peoples or Chief Oshkosh – while checking out the dance floor below.

The Eagles had two closely guarded entrances to the ball-room where the receptions were held, but because of the movement of guests and the wedding party between the ballroom, the bath-rooms, and two other rooms on the main floor, we occasionally entered with the flow.

There were other underhanded ways of intruding on these pri-vate affairs. One that often worked, but not to be overused, was reciting the names of the two getting married to the one on duty and then convincing him that we were simply reentering the hall from the men's room.

But the Eagles, determined to close the doors to gate crashers like us, began ink stamping the invited guests which brought an end to this chapter in our lives.

Card Playing at the Cellar Tavern

Card playing was a staple of our young years. Stakes were important. Somehow the idea of playing for fun did not appeal to us even when we played war on Aunt Elsie's and Aunt Emma's front porch when our age could still be measured in single digits.

We didn't wager money back then but there were other stakes to be risked that, at least at that age, were of equal importance. The currency, when playing against the four Hielsbergs, was one-up-manship, a badge of honor, carried by the winner for the remainder of the day.

Sheepshead became our favorite card game as we grew older. Games were organized at our house, at Schmittys, Burtons, Stein-hilbers, Tauschmanns, the Recreation Bowling Lanes, Menzel's Newsstand, and a few other places were cussing and a high level of concentration could be maintained.

Our favorite place during the later years of our young adult-hood was the back room of the Cellar Tavern. Gerry Steinhilber, Wayne Tauschmann, Lathan Burton, Darrel Schmidt, my brother Bob and I were the regulars. Honey and Gordy Hielsberg, Wiener Gruhlke, Don Polfuss, Wayne Reese and brother Rich were the fill-ins. The stakes were five, ten, fifteen, double on the bump. We built pots, didn't play leasters.

We were serious when we took our seats. The amount of money intensified the competition and sometimes tempers flew, most often when a player disregarded one of Hoyle's rules. $5 made a lot of noise in 1955.

It's still easy to picture the six of us sitting around this wooden table in the back room of Carl Dreyer's Cellar Tavern ordering our taps, putting change on the table, and dealing out the cards. The seriousness of the moment and the anticipation of competing were not always tempered by our friendship and our mutual affection. Emotions were not checked at the door, so we found out a lot about each other, sometimes more than we wanted to know.

The smugness in Wayne Tauschmann's smile when he was winning was constant on these Saturday afternoons. So was the tossing of cards in a fit of disgust when losing a hand he expected to win. The impetuousness of "Smiley Riley", a moniker poking fun of his surly personality, was a spur-of-the-moment outburst that we knew would soon pass unless another unfavorable situation arose.

When the tension became intolerably thick, which it often did after some poorly played hands, Steinie, in an effort to break the ice and calm the waters, would, in his low-key way make some innocuous comment, belt out his full-grown laugh which, in too many instances, prompted Tausch, sensitive as he was, to get up from his chair, say his pet line and leave for the day.

My brother too was not immune from such eruptions. We could count on Bob in a close game on a bad afternoon scattering 32 playing cards in a burst of anger and then, with the gusto of a drunken sailor, deliver the magic of six words his parents and future wife would not have been proud of.

The rest of us, outwardly at least, seemed to accept the turn of events more philosophically.

When the game was over most of us left for the comfort of our homes. But for Bob and Schmitty life on those Saturday nights was pre-planned, pre-arranged. Down to the T&O Bowling Lanes to meet Diane and Cathy, discuss the evening's calendar over a few brandies and water, and then out of earshot and eyesight of their dates the two would flip a coin to decide the pairing for the evening ahead.

No one usually lost a lot of money on those afternoons of tipping beer and playing the game we loved. Occasionally it happened, but the amount was never a crippling one. It was the camaraderie that brought us together. We joked, laughed, swore, drank, and competed as best as we knew how.

What better to ask of a Saturday afternoon.

Cherished Friends and
Extraordinary People

Top photo: Floyd "Ducky" Driessen of the T&O Bowling Lanes. Middle photo: Paul Schlindwein, Mike McMahon, Bill McCarthy. Bottom photo: Lathan Burton, Bob Hielsberg, Jim Last, Darrel Schmidt, Wayne Gruhlke

Fred and Erna Ploetz

The corner grocery store was one of the neighborhood fixtures when I was growing up, a place as ubiquitous as the corner tavern, the neighborhood school, the nearby church.

There were 16 of these small, mostly family-owned stores within 5 blocks of where I lived, each with its own personality and most located on a corner. None of them remain today. None of them. They simply could not compete with the prices, the selection, and the variety larger food stores offered. So they went the way of the horse and buggy and black and white TV.

They were viewed as much as a social center by the customer as they were viewed as a business by the owner. There was a humanness there, a neighborliness that did not exist in the larger stores. It was a place where you sat and visited with friends and with the owner when he was not busy tending the store. It was a place to drink a pop, eat a candy bar, and, after your grocery list was filled, say to the owner: "write it up."

My mother did her weekly shopping on Fridays at Krogers, a south side supermarket, when their advertised specials competed favorably with Krambos and the A&P, both downtown stores. Even though the bought groceries would fill, sometimes spill-over the kitchen table upon her return, the supply, with 6 boys and 1 husband to feed, would not last much beyond the weekend.

The fill-ins: the loaf of bread, the quart of milk, the pound of butter, the ring of bologna, the items a family needed to carry them through to the next Friday were bought during the week at the corner grocer. And, if you had a sense of loyalty, you bought them at the one in your neighborhood.

In our neighborhood the store was Ploetzes.

The owner of this store with a concrete step walkup was Fred Ploetz, who, along with his wife Erna, his son Harry, and Harry's wife Florence, and their two small children, Stevie and Joanie, resided in the same building.

It was not the best of arrangements.

I was sometimes sent there by my mother to buy a loaf of bread, a pound of butter or some other stop-gap staple she felt would be safe to buy. But it was mostly a stopping-off place on my way home from school or from visiting a friend or when I was bored and could not think of anything else to do.

I was on a first-name basis with the Ploetzes. I often "shot the breeze" with Fred and the Mrs., but usually I would just sit, have a pop, watch and listen, waiting for the social dynamics of this extended family to kick in.

Mr. Ploetz was Fred to most everyone, even to us kids, who frequented the place. He didn't seem to mind. He was, I suppose, in his sixties during my growing-up years, although to a youngster in his teens and pre-teens old was old. He was an easy-going conversationalist and a bit of a philosopher when the mood struck, but was also quiet and introspective when the strain of running the store became too much.

Mrs. Ploetz (she was the Mrs. to me as she was to her husband as in "The Mrs. is on a rampage again.") was a veritable dynamo. She packed into her small frame a force of energy that in its directness knew no bounds. When she was angry she was unrelenting in her verbalness as if on a mission to exact the full price of the wrath she so often carried. She could be soft and caring too, but not when she carried the banner: "Protector of the Brood."

The weakness of the mother was in spoiling.

Harry was the only child of Fred and Erna and despite his age and having a wife and family, he remained stuck in the early stages of adolescence. He was not allowed to grow up, to take on responsibility, to fail. He was not held accountable for his actions.

The Mrs. still coddled Harry at the age of 35.

Harry, who could usually be seen in-and-around the store when he was not drinking had a bad work history. He had a hard time holding down a steady job due to his drinking and his inability to take orders. His lack of independence and lack of a steady income was the source of many arguments between father and son.

Ploetz's Grocery. This is a young Fred and Erna Ploetz. The boy is Harry. I'm not sure who the girl is. The photo appears as if it was taken 20 years before we moved to the neighborhood in the mid-1940s

It was not always an idyllic place to be.

The relationship revealed itself in ways familiar to fathers and sons who become alienated. But in one way, clearly apparent to anyone who made a purchase in the store, it took on an unconventional, even bizarre form of conduct although to those unaware of the social dynamics of the place, a connection between father and his aberrant son may not have been made.

It was Fred's new system of money management.

His garb – a pair of pants and a vest with four pockets – was his modus operandi. He kept quarters in one vest pocket, half dollars in another, and dimes and nickels in the remaining two. The folding money – dollars and five dollar bills – were kept in his two front pant's pockets. The big money he placed in his wallet, and his wallet usually bulged.

The pennies were left in the cash register.

He did this because his son, when in need of money, would simply help himself to the contents of the cash register and use it to go on a toot. When this easy access to his drinking money was stopped, Harry's temper fed on his need for escape. And at those times his rage would quickly and predictably be picked up by his mother's antenna.

Whatever the Mrs. was doing, it was quickly put down.

I can still see her coming from the back room, housedress and apron on, rayon stockings rolled halfway to her knees, slippers too big for her feet, walking her walk – it was actually a fast shuffle as she tilted from side to side – until she was right over Fred who was usually sitting in his black leather-like rocking chair at the rear of the store.

With her finger rocking back and forth as she pointed, she would scold Fred about his tightness, his lack of trust in his son, his unwillingness to let Harry assume more responsibility in the store's operation.

Her bombastity was unrelenting. She was loud, and she was persistent. He didn't stand a chance.

Fred usually stayed and took it.

He wanted to escape the anger of his wife but also wanted to be in the store for his customers. The intricacy of the situation was his fear that Harry might keep the money if he was not there, and, even if at times that did not matter, unless the customers had the exact change Harry could not successfully make the transaction.

Sometimes it seemed that nothing mattered. The incessant nagging and the temper outburst would take their toll and Fred had to get away.

But the choices of escape were limited to this store owner past his prime. Sitting by his garage or walking in his garden were his usual choices. But the lot was small and the distancing thin, and if the anguish was deep enough and thick enough I might see him walk across the street to the corner tavern to hoist a few. At least he had someone to talk to in there, someone who might lend an understanding ear, someone who would nod in agreement to his complaints about "this whole damned situation."

If all this was not enough the rest of the family treated the store as their own pantry. They seemed to take what they wanted without regard to hygiene and good business practice. Fred sometimes put his foot down but usually backed off realizing that the strain of arguing and getting upset was too high a price to pay. It was easier to sit in his old black easy chair reading, snoozing, often just staring off in space.

His thoughts were his own.

Nothing seemed to bother him then. Maybe it was his way of shutting out the outside world. Even when Joanie and Stevie were running between the kitchen and the stairway leading to the upstairs and the Mrs. hollering, oftentimes cussing, frequently in German, for the kids to come back and finish their suppers, Fred remained composed.

It all seemed so strange.

Mother was reluctant to shop at Ploetzes. She knew too many people were handling the food, and too few people were shopping there. "Make sure it's fresh" were often her parting words as I headed off across the street. And when she needed sandwich meat for packing lunches, she put me on notice that Mr. Ploetz was to use the meat cutter and not his knives to cut slices from his loaves of meat.

"He cuts too thick."

And the store was dirty. Most every can or box of food sold, when taken from the top shelf, was thick with dust. Fred would sometimes blow the dust off the top of the container before wiping it with a cloth hung nearby. If the cloth could not be found his sleeve would do. "That won't hurt a thing," he liked to say.

My mother simply would not go in the store. We bought a few things there only because of Dad's insistence. Loyalty was important to him.

"You're a good boy Ronnie," the Mrs. would sometimes say when her thoughts were on a few of the older kids who helped themselves when they thought the Ploetzes were not looking. It made me feel good when they took me in like this.

Later on I realized that, like most families living under strain, the Ploetzes went about their business and stayed in their own world as much as they could. They made their way and lived their lives as many of us do today. But to a young, impressionable boy, this family, this place on the corner, unlike all of the others, left its mark.

I still think of Fred and the Mrs. and Harry and the kids. I think of the store and the dust and dirt, the voices in the back, and the smell of supper on the stove. I think of Fred's hand-driven meat cutter and sharp knives, his empty cash register and pockets full of money. I think of his bulk cookie display and his old-fashioned refrigeration system, his large magnifying glass and his clock repair station. And I think of the few regular customers who shopped there out of neighborhood loyalty, and of Dad who became a friend of the Ploetzes; all of them.

Above all else, what I think of when my mind turns to the corner of 12th and Minnesota is a place where I could go, drink a pop, sometimes "chew the fat" with Fred and the Mrs. or just sit and while away time before I headed off across the street.

Ole Menzel

He owned a small, notion-type store and newsstand on Eighth near Minnesota Street close by to the 20 or so of us south siders who too often considered it our private domain.

We met there during noon hour and after school, and sometimes on Saturdays when there was little else to do. We went there because it was a place to be with friends, drink a pop, and play some cards.

The owner, Ole Menzel, drew his profits mainly from the sale of newspapers, magazines, greeting cards and the like, purchased primarily by adults who came and went. He also sold candy, peanuts, chewing gum, and pop, teenage staples. The candy, peanuts, and gum were behind the counter. The pop was self-served from a cooler a good distance away.

There was an honor system at work here and, under the watchful eye of Mr. Menzel, it mostly worked. But there were a few whose adherence to the principle of fair play wavered at times. Their pilfering, that seemed funny to the wrong-doers, did not set well with the rest of us. When the guilty were caught as they usually were and asked to leave – barred from the premises for a short period – we were pleased. When the miscreant asked to be readmitted, Mr. Menzel, after giving the requisite warnings, would allow the perpetrator to come back into the fold.

We did more than drink Pepsi and eat peanuts at Menzels. We played cards, sheepshead mostly, in the corner of the store near the soft drink cooler. Although Ole, as he was affectionately known by the regulars, did not furnish a table and chairs for our use, we improvised by using empty wooden soft drink cases stacked nearby. Whenever we stayed more than the usual 15 to 20 minutes the odds were better than even that a game was in progress.

The money we spent in this place was minimal in the overall scheme of things. I usually bought a Pepsi or a Royal Crown and a bag of Planter's peanuts. Cash outlay, 10 cents. Later pop, for a 12 ounce bottle, would increase to 6 and then 7 cents. Most everyone spent the same kind of money.

It was at Menzels that I first learned to put the peanuts in the Pepsi. The salt of the peanuts cut down on the carbonation and gave the pop a slightly different taste. And it was fun, the novelty of it, eating peanuts from a bottle.

A large part of our group was made up of the Zanders, the Stuebers, the Werners, the Tollards, and the Ternes. And the names of Hielsberg, Gruhlke, Tauschmann, Steinhilber, Dahlke, Reese, Schmidt, Westphal, Demler, Wokosin, Langkau, Molash, Kempinger, Raddatz, Drumm, and Patten, all solid south side names, pretty much rounded out the crowd.

Allan Langkau was our designated leader and our liaison when a problem developed. When our language and behavior got out of line, which it often did, Allan would tell us to tone it down before we were all thrown out. At other times, when Mr. Menzel's feathers were ruffled it was Allan who did the soothing, the care-taking.

The pace was not always hectic at Menzels. Sometimes there were just a few of us in attendance. And, for reasons still unclear, if we were just sitting around doing nothing but drinking our Pepsi with the peanuts inside, we might find ourselves coloring our dialogue by attaching the word baby at the end of everyone's name, as in Wiener-baby or Honey-baby. I might say, if Wokosin and I were there alone waiting for others to show; "Hey, Eddie-baby." Eddie would replay in kind, "Ronnie-baby." That was it. But it was always good for a few laughs and it passed the time.

My time at Ole's ended in the summer of '53. High school was over and a 50 hour work week occupied most of my time. But I did see Ole now and then, mostly at Mike's Grill eating his evening meal. He was friendly when he saw me, acknowledging my presence with a wave of the hand and a smile.

I can not recall thanking him for putting up with all of our silliness, our misbehavior, and the disrespect a few showed towards this man old enough to collect an old age pension. I should have. It meant a lot to us, to me, to have a place like Menzels, a few blocks from where we lived, to meet, to enjoy each other's company, to just be kids.

Minnie Wegner

I seldom thought of her when looking back with others at our junior high years. The talk usually centered on our coach and friend, Marty Anderson. Other teacher's names were brought up, stories told, incidents remembered, but yet, she rarely crossed our mind, my mind.

But time has its own way of sifting and sorting, and she has appeared more often of late, sometimes out of the blue, but mostly when I'm alone and deep in thought. And I think I know why.

She was different from the others: quiet, soft-spoken, disarming, and very gentle. Unlike many who taught by command, or who were uncomfortable with 30 restless, sometimes inquiring, mostly mischievous teenagers just entering a period of life they had no preparation for, this tall, plain-looking, and thoughtful woman was ideally suited for the job.

She may have passed as ordinary to many, but to this 13 year old she was unusually perceptive and pleasantly helpful. A grandmotherly sort who took time to help, to listen, to fuss over you, which, of course, was the secret wish of every youngster lacking in grace and making mistakes. She entered my life at just the right time. I've always meant to thank her, but, like many things, I never got around to it.

Several years ago I was asked to help eulogize one of my former junior high school teachers. I was nervous that evening knowing I would appear in front of some of those who, some 30 years before, had intimidated me with stern looks and strong words. And when I arrived and saw most of them in attendance the timid child in me reappeared. When my turn came to be introduced, my mind, now only registering fear, suddenly turned to mush. The notes I had made no longer played that melodic tune of the night before. I was in shambles when I got to that podium.

Somewhere in that short and scattered discourse of mine, I spotted this almost-forgotten face with that same comforting smile, waving softly and voicing my name for only my eyes to hear. I stopped whatever I was saying to acknowledge her presence and my considerable feelings for her without trying to distract from the guest of honor. Her presence got me through the rest of my notes.

In the newspaper today I read of her death. I was saddened, but mostly I felt guilt; a failure to tell her how important she was in shaping this boy of so long ago and gently nudging him in the right direction.

Edward A. Koch

My mother, who grew up in a Lutheran household, took comfort in her faith. Her parents were devout Lutherans and her paternal ancestors emigrated from West Prussia to escape religious persecution.

My Father, on the other hand, having two grandfathers that left the Catholic Church, grew up as a part-time Baptist. Whatever his religious training, his church-going after he married, did not seem as important as sleeping-in on Sunday mornings.

Mother, fully understanding her husband's frivolous approach to organized religion, insisted, soon after her fourth son was born, that the family join the religion of her youth so her children could get the proper religious training.

Knowing Mother's determination and her stubbornness (he called it her Deutch temper), Dad more than likely had little if any resistance to a change having little import for him. With a religious heritage preserved, our family now attended church one block away.

The church was First English Lutheran pastored by the Reverend Edward A. Koch, a forceful, no-nonsense preacher whose sermons were tedious and long. On those Sundays I sat in the choir loft I rarely listened, preferring my own wandering thoughts, which were considerable back then, to the weariness brought on by my attempt to understand his message.

Religious instruction in Reverend Koch's church soon included catechism classes for those of us entering seventh grade.

The class met on a weekday after school and on Saturday mornings with our pastor emphasizing the need for perfect attendance. I played football and basketball at South Park during this time and, as it was bound to happen, practices occasionally conflicted with religious instruction.

It was in the fall of our last year of class when Donnie Laatsch and I decided after considerable deliberation and a good degree of uncertainty to attend football practice rather than attend the late afternoon instruction. We did not yet know what it meant to cross paths with the Reverend E. A. Koch.

We later learned when E.A. asked the class where the two of us were, one of our classmates, who knew, told. So the good Reverend sent this blabbermouth three quarters of a mile to bring the two of us back. When the snitch talked to our coach, fear rushed through our bodies faster than our left halfback, Wayne Reese, darted through the hole off-tackle in the previous week's game against the tough west siders from Roosevelt.

Coach Anderson, having had past experiences with the Reverend, told the two of us to report to catechism class.

Slowly and reluctantly, and trying along the way to think of some half-way reasonable excuse for our absence, we walked to a reckoning we knew we couldn't adequately prepare for. We were hoping class would end before we got there.

As we carefully entered the back door of the church annex, quietly closing the door behind us, we heard the thunderous and authoritative voice of our pastor: "Where were you two?" Forgetting any excuse we thought along the way we slowly tried to disappear in our seats. With a long pause for effect, long enough for the two of us to wallow in our guilt, he announced to the entire class that: "because of the lateness of two people, classtime will be extended."

Near the end of our religious instruction, the good Reverend asked each of us to attend and to observe Holy Communion before our Confirmation Day. Donnie and I, not wanting to provoke the ire of our minister again, and wanting to show that we took our commitment to the church seriously, attended Holy Communion services the Sunday following his announcement. But since we processed only half his message, we would soon be reminded of another ecclesiastical blunder.

Confirmation class of 1950

On that Sunday after the regular service was over and the communion songs began, the two of us were getting ready for adulthood at the corner of Eleventh and Minnesota.

We were sitting in he middle pew on the left side of the aisle when the two of us noticed, as the ushers were directing the people in front of us that our classmates, who were in attendance, remained seated. Although this gave us pause, we reasoned that they were watching how it was done and would participate at a later service.

We didn't know they had listened and understood.

So when the usher got to our pew, Donnie and I, with the thought of earning our pastor's respect and gaining his forgiveness, got up and walked to the front of the church were the communicants were lined up to receive the body and blood of our Lord

Jesus. While we were standing at the Eucharist table, a number of adults about to receive the consecrated bread and wine looked at us strangely.

When the Reverend came around with the unleavened bread and saw the two of us near the end of the receiving line, he gave us that look and passed us up with the Body of the Lord. Likewise with the wine.

Despite those slip-ups my years at First English included more than mistakes of judgment and ecclesiastical missteps. It was Sunday School and Summer Bible School, Father and Son Banquets, Junior Choir, Easter Service, and Christmas Programs, and that sense, that feeling of belonging to something greater than self.

Best remembered was the Children's Program performed on Christmas Eve. They were fun and light-hearted for the adults, but scary for the grade schoolers who gave their recitations standing by themselves in front of a packed church. The timid voice, the forgotten lines, the tears were as common as those whose pieces were recited with a clarity not commonly associated with the early elementary student.

With the program complete, each of us, who took part, lined up to receive our Christmas gift: a bag filled with one Red Delicious apple, one Navel orange, one popcorn ball, an assortment of nuts, and a variety of Christmas candies.

To a child who grew up in a family where money was scarce and Christmas lean, this gift shines the brightest when I think of that church on the corner of Eleventh and Minnesota.

Epilogue

My wife and I and four of my brothers and sisters-in-law attended First English Lutheran's 100th Anniversary celebration in June of 2007. With the exception of my parent's funerals it had been close to fifty years since I last attended the church of my youth.

Changes had occurred. That I noticed. Gone was the elevated pulpit where Reverend Koch oversaw his flock. The current pulpit, when the minister was not moving about administering the faithful – a change, I believe, Reverend Koch would not have endorsed - was now on the same level as the sitting congregation. The choir loft was located on the upper level in the back instead of in full view of the parishioners, and the wooden pews, on which I squirmed, wiggled, and fidgeted years ago, were now generously cushioned.

When the opening hymn "I Love to tell the Story" was sung, my thoughts drifted back to this church on the corner, and to Reverend Koch, and to a mother who loved singing the old hymns. I stayed there for a moment, immersed in this almost forgotten landscape of my childhood, and then, as I awoke from this quiet reverie, I felt the presence of my mother. It was very clear to me that she was there. Perhaps I was still deep in thought, wrapped up in a time my mind turned to minutes before. Maybe I simply wanted her there, but she was there. Of that I'm sure.

Later that day, after enjoying a noon brunch in the church's auditorium and listening to those who spoke of the church's history, my wife asked what it was that so moved me in church, even caused me to be a bit teary. I told her.

100th Anniversary of First English Lutheran Church

As I sat reading the anniversary program, mindful of my mother's presence and listening to the sermon preached by the Reverend Robert Herder, I was having difficulty reconciling Reverend Koch as anything but a hard-nose, forceful, no-nonsense preacher of the bible against the portrait drawn of the one who headed this church for forty years.

To be told he was a fullback on the football team and a center on the varsity basketball team at Luther College went against everything I believed. To picture the Reverend I knew doing those things kids and young adults often do was outside the scope of my experience. Any minister of the gospel, especially this highly disciplined, inflexible Reverend of mine, would be too proper, too dignified to play sports. And even if he did, although that perception was incompatible with my notion of ministers of the gospel, why would he send a fellow classmate, three-quarters of a mile to drag the two of us away from an important football practice.

When the service ended the congregation slowly filed into the auditorium for the catered brunch. As I walked through this narrow corridor separating the church and the auditorium, pictures of the confirmation classes of the past 100 years were on display. When I located the class of 1950 and spotted that boy in the second row, I thought of this self-absorbed teen who had not yet acquired a wider perspective on life and reminded him that this man, this reverend of his, had a greater influence on his life than he once wanted to admit.

Friends at the T&O Bowling Lanes

The feeling coming home is no longer there when I drop in and have a beer. Too many years have past, too many unfamiliar faces when I look around. And when I sit and watch in my aloneness sentimentality stabs at me, and I soon find myself getting up to leave.

It wasn't always this way.

It was in the fall of 1948 when a bowling alley with 16 lanes, a substantial number for the times, opened its doors for business. It was built on the corner of Tenth and Oregon with Rothenbach money replacing what was once a grand, stately house with a third story cupola that had, over the years, fallen into disrepair. Taking its name from its location, the T&O soon became a nightly destination.

There are places when you're young that feel more like home than home does. For two of my brothers and me, and many of my friends this place was the T&O.

It was something about bowling and the sound of echoing pins that drew us there night after night. Most any game played with a ball drew our attention. So it seemed natural for many of us to take to bowling and to this place that lured people sharing the same attraction as us.

This particular place had more going for it than bowlers and bowling alleys. It was new, and large, and inviting, and served as a collection point for many of us who were young and looking for things to do. And there was work to be had, an opportunity to exert a degree of independence that 14 and 15 year olds yearn for.

But it wasn't the lure of bowling and work that is best remembered about this place housing a restaurant that grilled the best hamburgers in town. It was its cast of characters still talked about with a fondness that has not faded with time.

Arno Abraham, who married into the Rothenbach family, was the owner and manager of the operation. He was known to run a tight ship carefully watching the nickels and dimes. When I graduated from working in the pits to working behind the bar, he was emphatic that I was not to get in dice games with the paying customer.

Arno was a business and ledger man. When he realized that this new and expensive building was only bringing in revenue eight months of the year, he decided to correct this undercapitalization.

In the summer of 1953, a new dance hall opened in Oshkosh.

Arno, at the end of that bowling season, went to great expense to install a large, portable wooden dance floor constructed over the entire 16 lanes with plenty of room for hundreds to dance without the slightest chance of bumping into each other. He hired Ron Harvey, a then popular dance band from Fond du Lac, to play the opening night hoping for a big inaugural turnout.

There were, counting the bartenders, about 25 in attendance.

The concept of year-round revenue was soon abandoned by this owner whose ledger books soon turned the color of red.

There were others of different colors that assembled on any given night. Opie Below with his snow-white hair was the most loyal of the many steadfast T&O regulars. He was often overheard in his wheezy voice, when he was too excited to unpocket his mechanical vibrator (he had cancer of the larynx), mouthing "pissball" and pointing in his mocking gesture with his stub hand and waving his other arm in disgust to those not properly stroking the ball into the pocket.

There was Mebs Luedtke, the maintenance man, who oiled the alleys the old-fashion way with a spray gun and a mop rag; Marv Fritz, a young and naïve 18 year old from Milwaukee, the clean-up guy and the one Arno took under his wing; Joe Ratchman, their long-time bartender and official greeter, had a good word to say to most everyone; Latto Gluth, working the counter and, during

The lounge at the T&O Bowling Lanes

the fifth frame beer rush, behind the bar, liked his beer warm without foam, and; Claude Rothe, a bartender, and an ignorer of Arno's many dictums, was the unofficial storyteller and entertainer. His work station, as he defined it, took in a handful of sitting-down customers, much to the annoyance of Joe Ratchman who was constantly out of breath when the two worked together.

But the one still revered, the one for whom the bells still toll, the one for which we hold our glasses high, and the top honcho of this working brigade was Mr. T&O, Floyd Driessen, the alley manager. "Ducky", as he was known to most, became a friend and surrogate father to those whose spending money was earned setting pins.

"Ducky" protected his pinboys from the double-ballers and the tippers of the bottle when they insisted on bowling games into the morning hours. His paternal touch – sometimes not a gentle one, but most often a caring one – helped bring about in us a deep sense of loyalty to this man we had not yet gotten up the nerve to call "Ducky."

There was something about Floyd Driessen that is still difficult to capture in words. Maybe it was a wholeness that I saw, a completeness that warded off an all-too common human frailty of uncertainty. He might have been seen as headstrong and inflexible to those who didn't care for his straight talk and his unflinching comportment when he faced situations needing attending. That he seldom backed down many could attest to. His opinions and beliefs and sense of fairness never wavered. And this steadiness we found reassuring, although occasionally discomforting. We knew he was dependable, that what he said he would do.

There were others in this cast who are also missing when I journey there and it feels empty without them.

The old gang is no longer casting their shadows in this place that was once our stomping grounds, our second home. Nor are the Discher Brothers treating us to those old songs at the service bar on Friday nights. Mike Goerlitz is missing, so is Vern Zwicky and Bob Pribbernow. They and others like them helped give this place a feeling of kinship, of intimacy. You knew when you entered those doors on Tenth that you fit in, that you belonged, that you mattered.

Feeling detached and curiously out of place and longing for another time, I quietly lifted myself off the bar stool and began a slow walk to the front entrance that opens to an Oregon Street that has become a stranger to me as well.

Wayne Gruhlke

We met setting up pins, and hung out at Ole Menzels, the playgrounds at Jeff, and the grounds of the Oshkosh Country Club. I called him Wiener-baby, and he called me Lip and Ronnie-baby. We were the best of friends.

What we did was laugh. A lot. We laughed over silly things, sometimes over nothing. We would look at each other and just crack-up. This silliness usually continued until our sides hurt and jowls ached. And then, for no apparent reason, it would start all over again.

It was no different for others who knew Wayne. We all simply enjoyed his company. His light-heartedness and laughter drew us to him. He enjoyed life and when we were with him we enjoyed it too.

With his dark coloring, Wiener looked more Sicilian than his surname suggested. And he had those big hands that palmed a basketball at the age of 14 and a double-jointed thumb he often used to touch his forearm and then wonder, when he did this, why no one else could.

He had this peculiarity of looking from side to side a short distance in front as he walked, always intensely focused never uttering a word. It was disconcerting to those walking with him who expected some sort of chatter, perhaps a little conversation.

On one of those walks I asked why he did this. He said he was looking for loose change. If he did not have movie money or Pepsi and peanut money he would go for a walk. And he possessed this uncanny ability to find what he was looking for.

Like most in our crowd, Wiener, and I seldom strayed from

the straight-and-narrow. We smoked a little but never in front of our parents or older brothers. It was more teenage experimentation than rebellious activity. There were times we did things our parents would not have approved, but then so did most everyone else in those years of trial and error.

One such episode stands out. Nothing serious was involved. What it amounted to was finding ourselves in the wrong place at the wrong time, which, as most teenagers know, is not altogether uncommon.

We were standing, partially leaning on a wooden partition separating the bowling alleys from the bar area at the T&O, watching mixed keglers in a handicapped league trying to scratch out a decent score. Technically we were in an area restricted to 21 year olds, although it was common for many of us to stand there as it was close to the outside door.

As we were watching, biding time until one of us had a better idea for the evening, Sergeant Erv Behnke, the cop on beat, walked in and spotted us. In his gruff voice he said before we had a chance to turn around: "What are you two doing here?"

Caught by surprise and not able to respond he gave us a brief lecture about having to be 21 to be in the area, and warned us that he did not want to see the two of us in here again.

We went outside, walked around, not wanting to call it a night but not having the foggiest notion where else to go, what else to do. So after a few fruitless efforts to come up with something halfway appealing, we decided to head back to the alleys. What we thought we were doing was harmless and besides we set pins there and were friends with the alley manager.

We weren't there more than 10 minutes when we heard a familiar voice behind saying: "Okay you two, come with me."

It was Behnke.

We didn't know what he had in mind as he marched us a block away to the corner of Ninth and Oregon. But neither did we expect what was soon to take place.

A patrol car arrived a few minutes later. When Behnke opened the back door, we were instructed to get in. It was at this time I discovered that you can not open the back door of a squad car from the inside.

A few minutes later we pulled up in front of the police station on State Street.

I still remember an officer sitting at the desk on the right with two uniform cops standing along side as we entered the station. When the desk sergeant told Gruhlke, before we had a chance to get our bearings, that the detective was waiting for him in his office we knew this was serious business.

He motioned for me to take a seat.

Wiener was gone for a good half-hour when the sergeant told me to get up. As he led me down a narrow corridor, I saw this once perpetually-grinning friend of mine coming out of the detective's office with a look that spelled nothing but trouble.

As I entered the office, the detective asked me to sit in the chair positioned in front of his desk. Except for a small desk lamp that cast its glare at me, the room was dark. The two officers standing on either side of the detective gave me the once-over with their cop-like looks.

It was right out of the movies.

The one sitting behind the desk began the interrogation.

He started off by asking where I was that night at 8:30 P.M. I'm not sure what I said, but I was told my response was different from my partners. He kept up the query, often repeating himself in hope I would trip up, but when I didn't he told me my answers did not match up with my partners.

It was apparent not long into the session that he was getting impatient. He was not getting the answers he wanted. I did not understand, in my confused state, why he was pursuing this line of questioning when all along I was waiting to be chewed-out for standing in the bar area of the T&O Bowling Lanes.

After some 20 minutes the inquiry ended. Convinced we were telling the truth, the officer said they were looking for two boys who had broken into Vette's Sport Shop across the river on Main Street.

It was cold walking home that night. The experience was a sobering one so little was said along the way.

Another lesson learned.

Teenage years are mostly like that.

Bob Pribbernow

He was the loosest and funniest on this motley group of has-beens and wanna-bees that came together as a bowling team and the one who gave this team its personality.

Bob was in his 60s when I joined the team. Although past his bowling prime, he still outscored bowlers half his age. For years he bowled with a two-holed hard rubber ball, and despite the advances in equipment and design he continued to use the same antiquated equipment.

Bob was a World War II veteran who served in the Pacific. He was stationed on the Bataan Peninsula when the Japanese overcame the entrenched Americans in April of '42. Those captured were forced marched 60 miles under a hot, broiling sun with few rations to an interior railroad depot on the Philippine island of Luzon. Thousands were bayoneted, clubbed, shot to death, or simply left to die along the way. Those who survived were eventually placed on ships bound for Japan.

When he arrived in the Land of the Midnight Sun he was assigned, as were others, to a slave labor camp. Bob endured the wretched conditions, the suffering, the hard work, the limited rations and the lack of medical attention found in these camps. He seldom talked about those days and we rarely brought them up. Instead he drank rye whiskey straight up, water on the side.

Bob loved "putting people on." His story telling, though always in a tone conveying a certain seriousness, was riddled with hidden humor, exaggeration, a stretching of the truth that would make a charter member of the Liar's Club blink.

On our fist ABC bowling trip to Knoxville, Tennessee we traveled by car on a highway with the Smokey Mountains in view,

Bob began talking about the origin of the name given to these mountains that border Tennessee and North Carolina. His tongue-in-cheek explanation was getting the customary treatment from three of the four of us riding in the car that day – a smile, an occasional chuckle, an appreciation of his story-telling ability. The fourth, a fill-in, had not been around Bob that much and did nor know how to react to his ramblings.

Realizing he might have a gullible one, Bob shifted gears. Facing the three of us in the back seat he said: "You know, on these bowling trips we always take turns standing up so the others are able to stretch so that when we get to the tournament we're nice and loose. We always start with the person in the middle."

Not knowing if Bob was kidding, the newcomer, smiling uneasily, stayed seated.

"Seriously," Bob went on, "the muscles we use for bowling need to be stretched and exercised often. We found out unless we have enough room to occasionally do this on these long bowling trips our bowling is affected."

That was enough to convince our neophyte to begin his crouched stance as the car was moving toward Knoxville at 65 miles an hour.

There were other bowling tournaments – Syracuse, Dayton, Detroit come to mind. And the unexpected usually happened with Pribbernow along. Knocking back a few shots of rye whiskey while sitting on his bed undressed and blindfolded in a Syracuse hotel in the early morning after a late night out, because he didn't want to see his bloodshot eyes in the dresser mirror drew the expected laughs. And that time in Dayton when he stumbled over the foul line yelling that his finger was still in the ball as it was speeding down the lane (Bob was a butcher and had a few accidents at Buehler's Meat Market) had all eyes looking his way. Or when he appeared shocked and bewildered when the waitress in a downtown Detroit restaurant arrived with her serving tray piled high with an array of confectionary delights that Bob, with his Actor's Guild tom-foolery, had previously ordered. Or when he went on stage in a West Bend supper club and commenced to entertain everyone with his songs and glibness until the manager gently told him to give the microphone back to the vocalist who was being paid to entertain that evening brought about the usual mirth from his companions.

He knew his teammates were watching and enjoying every minute of his countless pranks.

Then we found out that there was more to this fun-living guy than we were aware.

We saw another Bob Pribbernow one night at his house, someone with a past so troubled, so painful, that he pushed it beneath the surface, covering it with his silliness, his fun-guy stuff and a fifth of rye whiskey during a night out.

He invited his teammates over for some refreshments on a Tuesday following a night of bowling. After some drinks, food and the usual bowling talk, Bob brought into the room a box filled with war momentos – letters, clippings, pictures and the like – and slowly began talking of his war experiences.

We sat there, mesmerized mostly, listening, watching, mindful of the seriousness of the moment. He told us about the march, the camps, his need to survive. We saw the sadness and pain when he told of his fellow prisoners dying from starvation and neglect, and then, when describing the homecoming that was virtually ignored because their grim experience was unpopular in the midst of the jubilant homecoming of millions of other American serviceman, he began to cry.

His recounting of these events, interrupted only with his ubiquitous back pocket handkerchief wiping away tears, was so shocking, so revealing we did not want him to stop. His wife, not wanting her husband to continue, asked if it would be better if he put everything away.

That night I came to understand Bob Pribbernow a little better. I came to understand the price he and others paid in places far from the comfort of my Minnesota Street home. And I came to realize that we seldom really know one another even when the other is a friend.

Bob is gone now. He died in his 80s some years ago. And that bowling team is now just a memory along with the quips and the odd idiosyncrasies of that two-fingered bowler with the knuckles on the first and third fingers missing.

"Well, if you don't have key lime, give me two pieces of blueberry a la mode."

Family

Top photo: Mother on her Confirmation Day. Bottom: Cousin Merle and
I sitting on my Uncle Dale and Aunt Jennie's car during the winter of 1938.

Memorial Day gathering by the band stand in North Park.

Dinner at our House

Dinner, the big meal of the day, was served at noon in our house. Five minutes after to be exact. If eating the heavy meal had its roots in farming and rural living when the sun was the highest and much of the work day still lay ahead, it also became the custom of working class families. If we were not in our assigned seats or close by when Dad arrived from his job at Buckstaffs, the chances of getting a fair share of hot food went down considerably.

There was no waiting for kids.

There were rules at our table, a protocol that was understood but not always followed. Food was passed from the oldest male to the youngest, meat first, then potatoes and gravy. The rest was up for grabs. When one of my brothers was out of order and got his fork in the way, Mother made the call. It was not always the best of times for the only woman in the household.

Mother seldom sat down with the family to eat. Her job, as she saw it, was to make sure the food was properly apportioned as it passed around the table. She juggled that assignment around helping feed the youngest and scurrying to the cupboard to cut more bread or to the refrigerator for a pound of butter, a quart of milk, or anything else asked or demanded by those of us gobbling up our food.

Mealtime for her was hectic. She relaxed only after all of us left the dinner table, which, as I remember, especially as the brood got older, was only 5 or 10 minutes after we sat down. If you were one of 6 boys you learned to eat fast. The pace of your eating was geared to those around you. There was dessert to consider and its sizes were not always the same.

Sunday dinners were always the best. We usually had roast chicken or roast beef; pork and beef when it could be found and afforded. Beef and pork were always served well-done, cooked through as the saying went. It was done this way because of unsanitary conditions that were sometimes found on farms and in slaughter houses.

Occasionally a hobo traveling from city to city would knock at our back door to see if we could spare something to eat. We later learned they knew, through a network of exchanges and markings made and passed on by those over-the-rail travelers, the houses that would not likely turn them away.

Mother, not being a stranger to those knocks on the door, would warm up the leftovers, usually potatoes and gravy, some vegetables and sit the man down to eat. She was not always comfortable doing this but she did it. She knew hungry, she knew poor, and she knew right from wrong. As Ma Joad said as the Joad family moved down Route 66 in John Steinbeck's The Grapes of Wrath during the height of the Great Depression looking for work: "I'm learnin' one thing good. Learnin' it all the time, ever' day. If you're in trouble or hurt or need – go to poor people. They're the only ones that'll help – the only ones."

Thanks to our parents we learned valuable lessons along the way. We learned that giving is better than receiving, and that the poor and the down-and-outers, as we once were, need help as they are there often through no fault of their own.

Dad and the Abels

Dad was not highly regarded by his mother-in law, Bertha Abel. It was apparent to most everyone that she was not fond of him and that her daughter had made a poor choice for a mate.

She always seemed on edge when our family came to visit and her anxiety seemed to grow arithmetically at the sight of his five boys. Five boys who were not always well-behaved. Five boys who liked to run, laugh, make noise, and get into mischief. Five boys who acted like, well, five boys. But it was my dad's outlook on life and his affair with the bottle more than the turmoil of five rambunctious grandchildren that doomed this relationship.

Dad was a laboring man and a Democrat, and if that was not discouraging enough, he considered himself a liberal who expected government to help the downtrodden, the unemployed, the homeless, and those who went without. So when Franklin Delano Roosevelt and the Democrats won the 1932 election he, like many, was elated.

Debating the condition of the working man was one of the joys of his life, and the debating halls of our father's world was the tavern where like-minded men could be found. The Irish in him made him a friend to all in these sometimes raucous surroundings.

But to the Abels' Dad was a talker, a dreamer, not a doer, and not, in their estimation, a good provider. So when Dad, in his not-so-well-thought-out-mind, brought up the subject of President Roosevelt with the Abels' excitement was seldom generated. Their taciturnity and German background did not allow this. There might be some nodding by Grandpa as he smoked his pipe, and Uncle

Clarence might say a few words in support of father's premises, but anything said was spoken without emotion and apparent conviction.

The Abels were not really concerned about the outside world. Their talk centered on family, children, garden, work, and church. Their German, Lutheran, conservative, rural, and hard-working background had already shaped them. They were taught to rely on their own wits and their own hands for success in this world. Your life is of your own making they believed. They were taught to accept adversity if they could not overcome it.

Their belief in Jesus Christ and his message were central in their lives. Faith alone would take them to the Kingdom of Heaven, and that Kingdom, with the glory of God, overshadowed what they considered slight inconveniences here on earth. God had his ways.

Dad with his New Deal and labor unions, minimum wage and guaranteed employment never stood a chance.

Tritt Family Reunion

It was the family highlight of the summer.

It began when family and friends gathered at the Tritt homestead in the town of Poygan to pay tribute to my great-great grandfather, William Lloyd Garrison Tritt, who volunteered to serve his country at the age of 43 leaving behind a wife and nine children to tend the farm. This small and intimate gathering took place two years following his release from a Confederate prisoner of war camp in June of 1865, and it marked the beginning of what would become the annual Tritt family reunion. It would be celebrated each of the next one hundred years.

An August, 1934 edition of the <u>Oshkosh</u> <u>Northwestern</u> imparted these words: "Believed to be without precedent in the city if not the state, the Tritt family descendents of the late William and Julissa Hubbard Tritt, held their 67th family reunion Sunday at Menominee Park here."

"At the reunion here Sunday, entertainment was furnished by Donald La Point and his Green Mountain entertainers, featuring old time songs. A vaudeville skit by Marjorie Knoll, Charles Flanigan, Irene Carpenter, and Dale La Point was also given which was followed by a resume of the Tritt family history by the past grand matron of the order of Eastern Star of Illinois, Eliza Varnell."

The reunions were large festive affairs when I came aboard. William and Julissa had 10 children and the summer gatherings of the family soon branched out to include such names as Knoll, Carpenter, Fuller, Blitz, Wilkerson, Flanigan, McRae, and La Point.

When I think back to these August gatherings, the sight of my two uncles playing and singing on the old park bandstand usually arrives first. Donald on the base and Carvel strumming the guitar played along with others in the 1930s, 1940s, and 1950s under the names of the Green Mountain Boys, the Texas Stompers and the Playboys, the latter having Sunday morning time on radio station WOSH in Oshkosh.

My uncles, who did much of the singing, had that down-home quality which gave their songs a pleasant, almost familial ring. Watching them in their cowboy hats playing and singing everyone's old-time favorites was the highlight of those summer reunions in the park.

All of Dad's brothers were self-taught musicians as was their mother and grandfather before them. Dad, the only one of six children of Madge Flanigan La Point not able to play an instrument, often aided a rendition with a pair of spoons. Music was an important part of the La Point family thanks mainly to their Flanigan roots.

The reunions of my youth didn't last long, but they did provide fond memories. They are memories of games and cousins and play, as well as running and exploring and enjoying the assortment of food family members brought, and then able to wash it down with all the pop we cared to drink.

Everyone brought their favorite dish. Asking Dad for some change to buy ice cream near the end of the day at Miller's Confectionary was a treat I was not ordinarily used to. Watching the entertainment, listening to the music, seeing the smiles of joy and contentment on the faces of adults, hearing laughter and kind words and feeling that you were a part of it all brought about a certainty of place and a sense of belonging that has stayed with me throughout the years.

The Tritt Reunion continued during the later years of my youth with more-or-less sporadic attendance. When Florence Wilkerson, the youngest daughter of William and Julissa, died in 1966 at the age of 100, this annual event faded into memory.

Two Uncles

They came from a family of musicians. Their grandfather Patrick Flanigan, was one of nine children born to Irish immigrants from County Cork. He was a fiddler and according to those who knew, would, at the drop of a hat, entertain anyone who would give notice. He liked to dance the jig while fiddling and, when his children and grandchildren were about, he would sit in his old leather-bound rocking chair and sing those Irish ditties transported from across the sea.

Patrick, along with his brothers Mike and Jim, and Jim's wife Sarah, organized the Flanigan Band. They performed at barn raisings, weddings, public dances and other social events in places like Poy Sippi, Pine River, and Orihula, small villages along the shores of the Wolf River and Lake Poygan in central Wisconsin. They were all self-taught as was Patrick's oldest daughter Madge who occasionally was asked to join this string quartet while still in her teens.

So when Madge's sons Donald and Carvel – two of the beneficiaries of the family's musical bloodline – decided, some years later, to form a band of their own it seemed like a natural extension of their musical heritage.

The played professionally in the mid-to-late 1930s under the name of the "Texas Stompers" and the "Green Mountain Boys" making appearances as far south as Texas and as far east as Pennsylvania. There was little money to be made during the lean years of the Depression running from one town to the next hoping to survive on small payouts, and in the process trying to establish a marketable name.

They sang and played those soft, down-home country and western songs which were popular then; songs that were pleasant and often laced with a touch of melancholy. There was sadness in what they sang. You could feel it in their voices, hear it in the lyrics.

But after too many years on the road trying to make it and suffering the likes of too many upstarts, the two decided to call it quits. They gave up their full-time guitars and bass fiddles to marry sisters in a double-ring ceremony.

The reality of the road gave way to the allure of settling down.

It was not long into their marriage that they realized music was central in their genetic makeup, that it needed an outlet. They told their wives they would still keep their jobs and play only on weekends, maybe during the week if work could be found.

They became locally known as "The Playboys" and before long gathered up playing engagements. A year or two went by when they were asked to play Sunday mornings on radio station WOSH.

The two continued with their part-time playing, enjoying some of the success they had hoped to carve out years before when suddenly and without notice it all stopped. Carvel, with his marriage in turmoil and in a state of disrepair, chose to run away, to disappear, to shun his family responsibilities. There would be no sign of Carvel or of his whereabouts for years other then his slipping in and out of the city one or two steps ahead of the law. It was as if he had disappeared from the face of the earth.

His mother, who kept a daily diary for over 40 years, recorded some anxious moments along the way. On May 13, 1960 she wrote: "It was quite a surprise to have Carvel walk in as we hadn't seen or heard from him in over five years." And on September 3, 1973: "Carvel's birthday, 59th. Have not seen him since May 1960." She learned, sometime later, that her third son moved to New York City, in Manhatten, after a series of intermittent stops along the way.

It was there where he came to the attention of the lunch-crowd in a Manhatten eatery. An article appeared in the <u>Manhatten Daily News</u> in June of 1981 entitled: "Sam, You Made the Lunch Hour Too Short." Pictured at the piano was her long-lost son, Carvel.

"The lilting melodies of the 1930s and 1940s flow from the keyboard of pianist Carvel La Point at Estoril Sol, a Greek-owned Portuguese restaurant" noted the article. "It's an embellishment that gives the garment people and other customers from around here a mini-vacation from the grind and tensions of daily work," said George Melis, the owner.

"It's a two hour musical trip into the past," my uncle remarked. "Some will tell me: Gee! I like that number. I haven't heard it for ages. And you know I haven't yet heard anyone complain."

After years of unfulfillment and years of running, Dad's younger brother finally found a warm, receptive home in the center of the Manhatten Garment District during the two hours of lunch trade.

With his kids now grown, Carvel began to spend more time in his hometown. During these occasional visits he was always asked to play and sing some of our favorite "oldies." It was then he reminded us all of times past.

Later on, this piano-playing uncle of mine was diagnosed with ALS, Lou Gehrig's disease. He lived out his final years, a random victim of this deadly, fast-moving affliction, far away in his Manhatten apartment.

In his last act of love Donald brought his brother's remains home where he was laid to rest alongside his La Point and Flanigan forebearers, reposed in the quietness of a cemetery on a hill within sight of his musical roots.

Twenty years later, at the age of 93, this bass fiddle player, who the old-timers said was the best around, passed on as well. His death put to rest three generations of family musicians and entertainers.

I can still see the two in their cowboy hats playing and singing everyone's old-time favorites at our annual reunions. Carvel strumming his guitar, singing in that nasal-twangy voice of his, and Donald easing in with his complimentary tone and pitch while fingering his bass fiddle brings back a time and place not easily forgotten.

Down on the Farm

L ike many small farmers experiencing the lean years of the Depression and the early years of what then was still a European war, Uncle Dale and Aunt Jennie decided steady pay in the city, as our nation geared up to defeat the Axis, was preferable to the uncertainty of commodity prices.

Although no longer farming the land, the family still kept a hen house full of chickens, an out building stocked with pigs, a small, unused milk house, a drafty, need-of-repair faded red barn with an adjoining empty silo, a few cows that were later sold, and an old beat-up plow horse that we rode Indian-style whenever the adults weren't looking.

Uncle Dale and Aunt Jennie had five children and my younger brother Ralph and I, who were compatible with their two oldest boys, Merle and Wayne, were invited for a week's stay, at different times, during summers of our youth.

It was during one of these early adolescent visits that Merle and I decided to go for a swim in the Fox River located about a quarter mile in back of their 80 acre spread. Although Merle had been warned never to swim there because the river was unsafe and treacherous, we decided, as only two 12 olds could, that this would make for a fun afternoon.

We chose a spot in the river that was narrow and not extremely deep. We intended to play this safe. After getting undressed – no suits of course, this was the stuff of Tom Sawyer, Huck Finn – we got into the family's rowboat, tied to a nearby tree, and began an experience that would be indelibly marked in our minds.

Our swimming consisted of diving into the water from the boat, paddling a few strokes and then to swim back to shore. This was just dangerous enough to make it exciting. Neither of us were good swimmers. We could dog paddle some, but our swimming skills did not include much more.

After one such episode, I looked down to discover a small black thing on my testicles. Merle told me it was a bloodsucker. His gruesome description of what might happen unless I promptly got it off was enough to throw a kid, a few years away from puberty, into a panic. I tried pinching and pulling but that didn't work. Merle said it would release its grip only if we lit a match to it. I continued using my fingers instead.

Merle, sensing my futility, retrieved a book of matches from his pant's pocket and lit one. He handed it to me, and, after a few too-careful attempts it dropped in the bottom of the boat.

We continued to stretch our limits not knowing a near disaster was waiting to happen.

I was the first to touch bottom and quickly ambled back to the shoreline when I heard Merle hollering for help. He had stepped into a hole – a dynamite hole we would later learn – one that was wide and deep. Each time he surfaced he would shout, grab his breath, go down, fight back to the top and yell for help.

I started to go back in the deep water but had difficulty paddling. My arms were tired and I was scared. I turned back to shore fully realizing what might happen.

My turning back, fortunately, was a blessing in disguise.

While Merle was shouting for help, an older neighbor boy, a Kriegel, was paddling his boat around a bend in the river, a distance of maybe 50 yards, when he quickened his pace after hearing Merle yell. I shouted every time Merle came up for air that someone was coming and not to give up.

We were in no hurry to return home that afternoon. We knew what might be in store for us. When we finally reached the house and opened the kitchen screen door, it was apparent by the looks on their faces that his parents already knew.

My brothers and I loved to visit the Omro farm. There were few farm chores to do and plenty of time to play, goof around, and lots of room to do it in.

We frogged, played in the hayloft, and shouted at the top of our lungs in the cavernous hollow of the empty silo, scooted the hens off their roost when retrieving eggs in the morning, threw empty corn cobs at the pigs just to hear them squeal, brought the last of the cows in from pasture, and pulled a teat or two and squirted milk at each other, "cooned" melons in the dark of the night from Kriegel's watermelon patch, and did those crazy things kids sometimes do when running loose on a farm.

But one thing the two of us never did again was venture back to the narrow neck of river behind their 80 acres of farmland to test the waters of the Fox.

Dad and FDR

Politics was the usual fare at our house on Sundays when company was over. It was a time when the men, over a few drinks, would argue the merits of our country's policies. Thriving in these sometimes strident surroundings were Dad and my Uncle Louie.

When those Sunday dinner meals were finished, Dad, ready to hold court, anxious to get started, was the first to get up for the comfort of the living room. The husbands of the women clearing the dining room table were already relishing the thought of another round of political discussion.

There were the usual preliminaries to deal with: work, weather, and the telling of stories told countless times before. It was only good manners. Like a fine wine before dinner, one's palate must be prepared.

When the small talk receded and a bit of anxiousness rushed in, Dad would be the first to speak.

"I remember (it was always 'I remember') when you didn't know where your next meal was coming from. Even when you had a job you could barely make ends meet. It's different today. The Republicans never gave a damn about the working man. All they cared about was the 'Big Shot,' the monied inerests. With Roosevelt in the White House the working man has the best friend he's ever had. And don't you forget it."

He always ended his declarations of political faith with: "And don't you forget it."

The main meal was being served.

Uncle Louie, with his usual bluntness, countered by uttering the unforgivable: "Hell, the New Deal is what's ruinng this country."

The red flag of politics was raised.

One could always count on my uncle saying this. He was a dyed-in-the-wool Republican who took management's side against the country's "creeping socialism."

"Who's going to pay for this?" was one of his favorite opening lines. Others, supported with plenty of anecdotes, real and imagined, were greeted with the same kind of contempt by the owner of the house.

"If the owners had their way none of us could make a living," countered Dad, his dander now up. "Roosevelt is for the common man, the working man, and it's about time more people realize this."

He too was not immune from exaggeration and fabrication when the moment called for it.

I was proud of my father who became easily stirred when confronted with dogmatic pronouncements from people trying to distance themselves from beginnings common to them all. In my dad I saw a man with feelings, a man with a common touch.

Uncle Ed soon got his say by talking about company loyalty and Americanism. Uncle Ed was a good foil for Dad as was Uncle Louie and Elmer Hielsberg, a former neighbor.

"<u>Reader's Digest</u> had an article on this just last month," Uncle Louie injected. "Some of these union officials are taking orders from Moscow, orders directly from the Kremlin. They're not concerned with the workers. They simply want to shut down this country. I think we better wake up to what's really going on," his arms now folded.

Dad, who was excitable, now became flustered. He was, of all those present, most capable of defending the "truth."

He reminded the three, while pointing his fingers, that they were nothing but common laborers, that the owners did not have their welfare in mind. He brought into the debate the Oshkosh Woodworker's Strike of 1898 and how George Paine, the owner of Paine Lumber, treated the strikers with contempt.

"They're no different today than they were back then. The communist talk is a red herring" he added. "The newspapers are good at this, Hell, they're all Republican anyway. Anyone with an ounce of brains knows this. And the <u>Reader's Digest</u> is nothing but

a right-wing, conservative, anti-Democrat rag that no self-respect-
ing working man should be reading."

He was worked up.

I was mesmerized.

Other stories were told with requisite interruptions and impa-
tience as more drinks were poured. But it soon became clear they
were beating a dead horse. Most everyone had gotten their licks in.
Their wounds – those that had not yet healed – might be mended
over a few drinks at the Cellar Tavern.

They left for the tavern two doors away.

I walked into the kitchen.

The women were playing Canasta and laughing. There was no
talk of Roosevelt here. Their laughter was light-hearted and warm,
their conversation soft. I enjoyed this and the fuss they made over
me. I felt secure, comfortable in their company. They were different than their husbands.

I stayed for a time just watching. Mother was smiling and
laughing, looking especially happy. I knew she enjoyed these Sundays. She loved the repartee these gatherings offered.

Her face glowed.

It was not easy, I thought, with five boys, a tight budget, and
a husband who sometimes drank too much. I loved seeing her this
way.

I stayed a little longer then wandered back to the front room
of an hour earlier. The excitement had stayed with me.

I was moved by the depth of feelings generated by their talk
of politics, and of Roosevelt and his New Deal. I was disappointed
that not all in the room were affected in the same way. I was glad
my dad came alive, and the one who became excited by events, by
men and their ideas. I wanted to be like him.

It was in school, some weeks later, when our fourth grade
teacher asked the class to vote in a mock presidential election of
1944. We voted by raising our hands. The Republican, Thomas
Dewey, won.

I sat at my desk in silence. In disbelief.

I waited for the teacher to scold. I fully expected her to
remind the class of the not-so-distant past, of the Depression

brought on by the party which Dewey represented. I waited for her to talk about the new opportunities for the working man, the bigger paychecks, and the enhanced self-worth. Surely she would remind everyone of their roots.

To my surprise none of this happened.

The rest of the day didn't matter to this boy who learned his politics at home. His mind was no longer on school. His thoughts were of his dad and on the "lessons of history."

He decided from that day on that he would defend the truth and carry the banner. His dad, he knew, would have wanted him to.

Father

I went to bed that night but didn't get much sleep. It wasn't the thought of boarding the Greyhound bus for my pre-induction physical in Milwaukee that kept me awake half the night. It was that conversation earlier in the day that I kept mulling over in my mind. I wasn't planning on what he said. I had already said my goodbyes. Now I simply wanted to slip away unnoticed, to be away from it all, to be on my own.

As the bus headed south the following morning my thoughts turned to my father and his attempts to talk, to say a proper goodbye, to make things right. But when he drove me to the station earlier that morning neither of us knew what to say. There was an awkward silence which reflected the distance grown between us. A dye had already been cast and the gloom each of us felt made the encounter as gray as the morning sky.

The chartered bus seemed to take forever to arrive while the two of us fumbled to keep this short visit a pleasant one. When it finally pulled in I turned to my dad, after giving my luggage to the driver, and saw this deeply forlorn look that made me feel guilty for being selfish, for being so protective of my feelings. I didn't know what else to do but to shake hands and board the bus.

The emptiness of that moment still haunts me.

The estrangement, this lack of closeness I felt with my father had to do with his drinking, and, I suspect, from his own childhood experiences.

My father drank heavy at times, and when he did, which was often in my younger years, he was incapable of being a father or a husband. He was considered an alcoholic by most everyone but himself. He took the "cure" when forced to, but the troubling nature of his inner being eventually required the healing powers of alcohol. At those times he drank compulsively, secretly, and in pain.

I can still see myself slipping into the garage as he tips back a pint of vodka or a bottle of beer. His Adam's Apple bobs, the liquid gurgles, he wipes the back of his hand over his lips, belches, and we both pretend the moment has not occurred.

He had difficulty, as fathers of his generation did, expressing affection. He was more comfortable with strangers and acquaintances than with his own family. He was apparently afraid of the closeness, the shared feelings, the intimacy family life offered. The guilt and emptiness he felt was met head on by his insatiable love affair with the bottle.

He's now been gone more than 20 years, and, with it, so has the anxiousness I often felt in his company when he was alive and we were alone. I see him clearer from this distance. The passage of time often does this. And I can see some of my dad in me much of which makes me proud.

There is never a finish to this, never a wrap-up. I suppose you could tuck it away in some corner of the mind but it would resurface with the need to be dusted off and reappraised once more.

It's like looking in the mirror and trying to figure out who that person is that is looking back.

Mother

It was on Father's Day, 1982, when a series of strokes took their toll on this once strong and healthy woman. Her family doctor said that she would not recover, that she would spend her remaining time in a nursing home without the ability to speak or fully understand.

We saw the anguish and the sobbing body during our visits and felt the desperation when she clutched our hands. We knew what she was thinking, what she was saying, but we felt helpless to intercede. When her final days were near we gathered around and said our goodbyes.

When the call came early that morning, I quickly dressed knowing that I wanted to be there to hold her hand one last time. To remember.

She was a farm girl, one of five born to hardworking first-generation German-Americans. She grew up a few miles west of Berlin, Wisconsin in the town of Fairburn on an 80 acre spread her father Paul Abel bought shortly before his marriage in 1904 to Bertha Schroeder. Her Prussian born paternal grandparents who migrated from Connecticut in 1882 owned a farm nearby. The church and one-room schoolhouse she attended for eight years were just down the road.

She wanted to continue her schooling but that was not a choice young farm girls in rural Wisconsin had those days. Our mother, as was the custom, had to choose a line of work, suitable for young, unmarried girls with little education. She chose to work in a glove factory in Berlin while boarding with a family during the week and coming home weekends to help on the family farm. She was all of 14

She moved to Oshkosh, a few years later, at the urging of her older sister, Hertha, who had arrived years before.

She started life in this city as a live-in maid with an Oshkosh family, and when an opening occurred, began work at Mondls', a shoe factory, and a place where her world opened to new friends and a future husband.

She married during a time when life for married women of working-class husbands was pre-planned and repetitive. Sameness was the common thread running through their lives.

Like most she dreamed of a home, a nice family. What she did not count on was being married to a man whose fondness for the bottle overcame, as Grandma Flanigan often pointed out, any good sense the Lord gave him. Over the course of 19 years of marriage, 6 boys were born to be raised with only occasional help from her husband.

It was not an easy life for this sometimes shy and introspective woman who grew old too fast. The old photographs tell the story. But she was one to hold her chin up and move on to the next day, while absorbing and too often internalizing the bitterness, the frustration, the disappointments her marriage brought. The problems, the sadness generated by those experiences were just below the surface and were easily tapped.

I often saw her wipe away tears with her apron while in the kitchen preparing food or dabbing her cheeks in the front room as she mended socks. Although she accepted her fate – she came from stock where individual pain and suffering were simply endured – she was not indifferent to it.

Her husband eventually retired and the two began to enjoy their golden years traveling, visiting, and enjoying their grandchildren. They worked in their church and took pride in each of their children. Life was good and they were content.

Then the unanticipated, the unexpected happened.

As I looked at her laying there, the warmth slowly receding from her body, I thought about this woman who gave her sons the direction and love they needed. I thanked her for being there, for her tenderness and warmth, for the strength in her large hands when she massaged my head and rubbed Vicks on my chest. I thought of those moments growing-up and being with her alone in that front room on Minnesota Street. I needed her then more than she might have known. I needed to hear her gentle and reassuring voice; I needed to feel her touch, see her smile, feel her warmth; I needed to know that I was important, that I mattered, and I needed her attention.

I assured her she did all of that and more.

As I gently laid her hand down to leave I thought wouldn't it be nice, one last time, to stand on the back porch of this house, open the door, and call out: "Ma, I'm home."

Closing

When I look back I still long for this period of life. This place, this community still exists for me. I still live in its ruins.

On those early summer mornings I stand at Boettcher's Phillip 66 Station at the corner of South Main and 13th Street hitching a ride to the Oshkosh Country Club hoping that Milo Miller and some of the other Sheepshead players are waiting in the caddy shack ready to get up a game. When I head out the door on my way to the school grounds, I wave to Fred taking in a breath of fresh air and see the Mrs. shuffling in her loose fitting slippers scurrying to examine the new growth in her vegetable garden. And when I arrive at school, a block and a half away, I notice my friends have not yet arrived.

I still feel the cold of winter in the mornings of our upstairs bedroom thankful that I still have on yesterday's socks and knowing Mom has already warmed the kitchen with a batch of hot cocoa on the stove and toast in the oven.

Seeing Teamer in our gravel driveway waiting for me to finish supper and hearing Mother asking whose turn it is for dishes before I silently slip away; watching Honky breakfast on a Bireley's orange at Diener's Grocery before traipsing off to start another day at South Park Junior High, and then, on our return home, stop at Week's Grocery to buy a banana cream center twinkie; riding recklessly in South Park with Jim Last who is determined to give the likes of Gruhlke, Reese, and myself a feeling that adulthood may never come; raiding vegetable gardens and fruit trees on warm summer evenings with little else on our minds and hollering, when

we were safely out of sight: "We are the Ready Raiders"; walking
that one block home after sitting through a four hour Sunday matinee wondering what school assignments needed attention only to
dismiss the thought as something to be done during Monday's
homeroom period; packing a big bologna sandwich topped with
yellow mustard and bike to the viaduct on 24th Street to watch the
trains cough up smoke as they make their runs through the under-
belly of that grassy knoll; taking my favorite shooter and a bag of
marbles with some aggies and crowbaits thrown in hoping to get up
a game down at the school grounds or in the dirt driveway or backyard of someone's house; throwing a tennis ball on the roof of our
house to get that certain bounce or hop, catching it in my glove and
then doing it over and over until Mother had had enough makes me
feel 15 all over again.

ndex

Printed in the United States
132811LV00002B/5/P